Decrypted is an excellent work by Hoe Lon that explains cryptocurrency from a traditional trader's perspective. The book provides sufficient knowledge for even newcomers to catch up with this seemingly complicated blockchain world without much technical background. I believe the book will help introduce more people to blockchain and cryptocurrency, an exciting innovation of the century.

Loi Luu
Co-founder, Kyber Network

I have always been a huge believer of inclusive finance, where the old and new economy find grounds to collaborate and embrace each others' presence. The first step is to educate ourselves, no matter at what career juncture we are at, and the remaining excitement of cryptocurrency and the sheer potential of blockchain technology will lead the way. *Decrypted*, as narrated by Hoe Lon, is the epitome of life-long learning and embracing of what disruption in his field has to offer.

Professor David Lee, Singapore University of Social Sciences
Co-founder, BlockAsset and Senior Advisor to Sentinel Chain

Decrypted is a trader's view of cryptocurrencies. A hard and uncompromising analysis of what it is, what it is not and most of all whether it will fulfill aspirations of what it can be. Hoe Lon has delved deep into the domain. *Decrypted* is certain to make an engaging read.

Wong Joo Seng
Founder and CEO, Spark Systems

Decrypted took me from the path of least resistance, blissful ignorance, to the path of blissful intelligence. Finally I truly "get it".

Jason Ambrose
Founder and CEO Vanda Securities

Shouldn't one take heed that this book is written by a seasoned money manager working in high finance, who, apart from his day job, pays acute attention to cryptocurrencies? I have not read any other books out there that has distilled the essence of blockchain and its philosophy in such an easy, accessible manner. Anyone wanting to have a good introduction to this fascinating world without feeling as though they are reading a textbook should pick it up. Anyone who wants to be reminded and re-energised as to why they got into cryptocurrencies in the first place should also read it. I know I did.

Kai C Chng
CEO, Digix Global

Decrypted shares an insightful narrative on the uprise of cryptocurrencies, providing a comprehensive view into the multifaceted interests of cryptoanarchists, bankers, and entrepreneurs. Hoe Lon outlines a thorough history of the blockchain ecosystem, and demonstrates the value of cryptocurrencies and blockchain technology for individuals and institutions. This book describes the potential impact of decentralised applications and provides a vision for how blockchain technology will come to be adopted.

Howard Wu
Co-founder, Dekrypt Capital

Bitcoin, Ethereum, Blockchain, ICOs: the cryptic world of cryptocurrencies is not only tempestuous but polarised. Perspectives are deeply entrenched with both support and opposition driven by almost cultish zeal. Cutting through that sound and fury, Leng Hoe Lon gives the uninitiated amongst us, a dispassionate framework with which to join the debate. He presents the concepts, their recent evolution, their promise and pitfalls in an accessible and engaging way. Using colourful analogies (such as an overbooked restaurant with decentralised management), Hoe Lon explains the mechanics of the underlying technology. Drawing from our experience with more traditional asset classes, he tackles the questions of 'value', 'bubble' and addresses overblown claims on both sides of the debate. *Decrypted* is not designed to be the last word for either enthusiasts or detractors. However, it is the first fair treatment of this field that I have encountered and should serve as a valuable point of reference for investors and regulators.

Lutfey Siddiqi CFA, Visiting Professor-in-Practice,
LSE Adjunct Professor, NUS Risk Management Institute
and former MD, UBS Investment bank

This book provides a great overview on cryptocurrencies and the blockchain industry. The mindset required to understand the fundamental change of the technology is well defined and expressed, which is the core component of conceptualising the benefits of blockchain in the future. A very good source to educate yourself on the subject.

Ronen Kirsh
Co-founder, Dekrypt Capital and Blockchain at Berkeley

DECRYPTED

A FINANCIAL TRADER'S TAKE ON CRYPTOCURRENCY

Leng Hoe Lon

Foreword by **Adam Levinson**

Marshall Cavendish
Business

Published by Marshall Cavendish Business
An imprint of Marshall Cavendish International

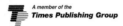

A member of the
Times Publishing Group

Other Marshall Cavendish Offices:
Marshall Cavendish Corporation. 99 White Plains Road, Tarrytown NY 10591–9001, USA • Marshall Cavendish International (Thailand) Co Ltd. 253 Asoke, 12th Flr, Sukhumvit 21 Road, Klongtoey Nua, Wattana, Bangkok 10110, Thailand • Marshall Cavendish (Malaysia) Sdn Bhd, Times Subang, Lot 46, Subang Hi-Tech Industrial Park, Batu Tiga, 40000 Shah Alam, Selangor Darul Ehsan, Malaysia.

Marshall Cavendish is a registered trademark of Times Publishing Limited

National Library Board, Singapore Cataloguing-in-Publication Data

Names: Leng, Hoe Lon. | Levinson, Adam, writer of foreword.
Title: Decrypted : a financial trader's take on cryptocurrency / Leng Hoe Lon ; foreword by Adam Levinson.
Description: Singapore : Marshall Cavendish Business, [2018]
Identifiers: OCN 1048626096 | 978-981-4828-70-3
Subjects: LCSH: Electronic funds transfers. | Money.
Classification: DDC 332.178--dc23

Printed in Singapore

Cover image by Aaron Gan (More on Aaron Gan on pg 165)

To all the traders in the world.
Yes, the machines are here to eat our lunch,
but they will never learn our gut instincts.
Don't stop believing.

This book is dedicated to you,
the reader—for taking a leap of faith
to accept the new world of cryptocurrencies.

CONTENTS

FOREWORD

When Hoe Lon approached me to give a Foreword to his book, the first thing I said was, "This is a fun project", and the courage to take a public stand on such a controversial topic is respectable. In the book, he applies his trading experience to demystify cryptocurrency trading.

Hoe Lon and I often discuss our global macro views, and cryptocurrency became a much greater part of the conversations over the last year. The traders in the financial world didn't care about Bitcoin until 2017. Mind you; the adoption is still pretty low. The parabolic price growth was a social phenomenon.

As a macro trader, I always evaluate various factors and put on a trade when a compelling opportunity arises. Several years back, when I was involved with Bitcoin at around $100, the bear thesis was around hacking of exchanges, links to nefarious activities and the 21st-century "tulip mania". On the other hand, the bull thesis was on three distinct arguments. First, a libertarian view on currencies free from government influence. Secondly, the discovery of digital gold. Lastly, the likely demand from China as a channel of capital outflow. The miners in China converted electricity to crypto that could be turned into foreign currencies outside of China, and everyone wants that. The rapid technological advances in the blockchain world were only the kicker to the long crypto trade.

Is it over? Emphatically no! History repeated itself when a futures market launch ended a strong rally. Bitcoin experienced that in December 2017, when many of the positions front running the event were liquidated. While you never know precisely where you are in a cycle, it is not over until crypto is institutionalised in some shape or form. Very rarely have I seen a cycle end with a narrow slice of participation. The hyper-realists are probably right that this market makes no sense, but be careful not to get stuck in an anchoring bias. It is hard and unlikely to be rewarding to fight the growing population's collective imagination. Most great trades are going with a major trend and sociological force.

The research team in my office calls this a Polymorphic Financial Instrument. It seeks to alter 5,000 years of global financial evolution, which tended towards increased centralisation since Hammurabi, King Croesus and more lately Bretton Wood. We believe the millennials will drive investment philosophy for the next two decades. The silent generation bought gold, boomers bought equities, genX put most in hedge funds, and millennials have already shown a distinct preference for digital assets.

This book is a great way to start your journey into cryptocurrency investment. Hoe Lon shares his fortunate experience and makes you understand from the financial trader's point of view. Whether or not you are involved already is not important. The decentralised revolution and the trust minimisation movement have many more chapters to play out. While this is by no means a comprehensive list, one should think about the following developments.

1. How utility tokens gain greater acceptance going forward.
2. The ETF-isation of cryptocurrency to allow older generation non-millennials to participate at ease and comfort.
3. The emergence of nationally sponsored fiat-crypto like the J-Coin ahead of the 2020 Tokyo Olympics.
4. The post regulation validation wave of adoption.
5. The institutionalisation of crypto assets that will come with the development of custody solutions.

This is too important as an emerging technology to ignore. Spending time is worthwhile. Hoe Lon's insight is a great aid in that exploration.

Adam Levinson
Managing Partner and CIO
Graticule Asset Management Asia (GAMA)

INTRODUCTION

CRYPTO AND YOU

> Television won't be able to hold on to any market it captures after the first six months. People will soon get tired of staring at a plywood box every night.
>
> —*Darryl Zanuck,*
> *Executive at 20th Century Fox (1946)*

Suppose two great financiers strongly disagree on some great new money product that's taking the world by storm—and they don't mince words. The first one (let's call him 'James') declares it to be "a fraud" and "worse than tulip bulbs," referring to the sixteenth-century 'tulip mania' in Holland.[1] James is so serious, he threatens to fire anyone in his bank caught trading in it. "It's against our rules, and it's stupid. And both are dangerous."

The second is a billionaire venture capitalist (we'll call him 'Timothy') who backed crypto from the very beginning, and sees incredible potential in it—so incredible, he's invested more than almost anyone else in its startups and exchanges.

"[It] frees people from trying to operate in a modern market economy with weak currencies," he has said. "We expect to be able to create new services that can provide liquidity and confidence to markets that have been hamstrung by weak currencies."

He's so confident in it that he buys massive quantities of it on auction for a few thousand dollars... and sees their value to grow to US$70 million over the mere three years he's held them.

Both James and Timothy have seen the trends. Both have presumably done the math. Both are responsible for the smooth transaction and use of billions of dollars ... and yet, they've arrived at vastly different convictions on the same issue. (Given their language and actions, I'm sure you'll agree that 'conclusions' is too weak a word.)

I haven't even changed their names. 'James' is Jamie Dimon, chairman and CEO of JPMorgan Chase. 'Timothy' is Bitcoin proponent Tim Draper, whose belief in its growing value over the coming years has led him to support crucial pioneering work in the creation and trade of bitcoins, such that each of them is worth thousands of dollars as I write this.[2]

What divides them—and millions of people worldwide—is a new way of thinking about money and its exchange.

The Name Is Currency, Cryptocurrency

Enter cryptocurrency, or *crypto* for short.

At its most basic definition, it's a financial product that, like stocks and bonds, doesn't physically exist; instead, it consists of a public record of transactions made, updated in real-time and secured using industrial-grade mathematical cyphers to protect it from being changed by anyone after the fact.

This immutable record, stored as a distributed ledger known as a *blockchain*, is entirely anonymous, with no personal information appended to it. This is where cryptocurrencies get their name; it's got nothing to do with mystery, unintelligibility or secrecy of any kind.[3]

I'll certainly admit that crypto is something of an odd duck, as far as investment instruments go. (For reasons I'll explain later, it's a slight misnomer. Crypto more resembles stocks and shares than it does the spendable, liquid money implied by the term 'currency'.)

For one, its creator was the first to lay out a system of money as a series of unchangeable 'agreements' between account numbers that would be stored in servers worldwide and synchronised regularly so that each had a ledger bearing the same 'content'... rather than assets held by actual, identifiable people.

He (or they) remains anonymous, going by the handle '*Satoshi Nakamoto*'—perhaps as a means of showing how you can hold large amounts of money in such an instrument, while remaining untraceable by banks, governments and other authorities.

He named it *Bitcoin*, and today it serves as the 'gold standard' for cryptocurrencies worldwide. Where once inventors sought fame, licensing fees and fortune, Nakamoto has gone the opposite route by avoiding media attention and paying himself in his own product.

Will cryptos like Bitcoin and its competitors (which we'll meet later in the book) go big and stay big, or flame out? Perhaps it's too early to say; as I write this, the concept of crypto itself is less than a decade old. That isn't a long time to hold a financial product like a stock, and the value of crypto could go in either direction.

But let me ask you a few questions. Would a poor investment attract so many startups, so much capital? Would it accrue thousands of dollars over a short time, such that what you spent on a pizza in 2010 would buy you a house and retire you for life?

(This has actually happened; in the first ever sale of something for bitcoins, programmer and Bitcoin enthusiast Laszlo Hanyecz paid 10,000 bitcoins for two pizzas on 22 May, an amount worth $5 million just four years later, and $20 million in 2017.)[4]

Personally, I knew that Loi from Kyber Network used his scholarship money to buy 5,000 ETH at ETH/USD 1.00 which he later sold for US$7,500 at ETH/USD 1.50, a 50% gain. Back then as a poor student, he was happy as he thought he had made some money. The value of his ETHs then would have been worth over US$3 million today!

Would important VCs like Draper pay much attention to it, much less fund it so thoroughly?

Would it attract committed users all over the world, and leave governments and banks scrambling to control pieces of the pie?

Would major banks like Goldman Sachs set up trading desks for it, and declare it a form of money to its clients?[5]

And would governments all over the world, including one that oversees one-sixth of humanity, get so heavily involved?

That hasn't just attracted dozens of startups to create literally hundreds of new cryptos, but also set up a market worth US$170 billion as of August 2017... and growing every day. Not bad for a concept that, as I write, hasn't even reached its ninth birthday.

Like the paper in your wallet, the data that makes up cryptos and their blockchains has no value in and of itself—it's only useful because everyone agrees that it holds some certain amount of value that can be exchanged for real-world goods and services. As of this writing, a single bitcoin is worth thousands of dollars, but this is because that's the average price across the various exchanges that dot the Internet.

As with government-issued currency (or *fiat*) it's not the dollar value that's important, but its buying power. There's no point in having hundreds of dollars if the necessities of life, like food, water and shelter, cost thousands.

The Reason For This Book

Why this book? Not because I want you to agree with me or anyone else, but to share the facts and why they happened... and only then invite you to decide whether cryptos like Bitcoin, Ether, Litecoin or something else are products you want in your portfolio. Cryptocurrencies are a completely new class of asset, built on technology that literally did not exist only a short time ago.

You may have heard of crypto before, whether in the financial pages; or when some criminal organisation threatened computer users worldwide and demanded ransoms in bitcoins. *That's* set off a firestorm of scepticism that I believe doesn't give crypto a fair chance. What if you or I missed out on something good simply because we believed its critics? There is no new invention under the sun that didn't have its share of them, and crypto is no different. I'm not going to sell crypto (or the blockchain technology it is built on) as the next quantum leap in finance, or otherwise dictate what you think about it. No one can—or should. But I believe that's a great reason to research the field for yourself, gather the facts and make up your own mind.

That said, some patience is needed as we tease out the intangible, uncontrolled nature of crypto. You can't see or touch it, and transactions work so differently in crypto that it looks like a whole new ball game.

That's why I wrote this book. I want to demystify the concept of cryptocurrency so anyone with no prior knowledge can understand how it works. I'll share how its decentralised structure works without the need for banks, government action or, indeed, verifiable authority of any kind—and show its relation to the real money we see and handle every day.

The fact that its creator is unknown, and its systems often invisible and unaccountable, doesn't have to be a barrier to your use and investment in it, any more than you have to know about internal combustion or who Henry Ford was every time you start your car. As the Bitcoin website puts it:

> Just like current developers, Satoshi's influence was limited to the changes he made being adopted by others and therefore he did not control Bitcoin. As such, the identity of Bitcoin's inventor is probably as relevant today as the identity of the person who invented paper [...] Nobody owns the Bitcoin network much like no one owns the technology behind email.[6]

I do this by sharing the 'pillars' of crypto operations, with an inside look at how new cryptos are planned, differentiated and sold, and what this means for the financial and political worlds... and by extension, you the individual trader and investor.

Like any specialised field, crypto has its own evolving 'language' that coins (no pun intended) new words and repurposes existing ones. I'll introduce new terms in italics, and give short explanations in the glossary at the end of this book.

Why Take Me Seriously?

I'm a banker and fund manager by profession, but have a keen interest in technology startups. While I got my start in Deutsche

Bank in 1997, I was told that foreign exchange trading (FX) would soon become obsolete.[7] I was still trading FX in JPMorgan Chase, ABN AMRO and Goldman Sachs through to 2011—but after managing fiat money in Tudor Investment Corp for five years, I grew more and more interested in ways to combine human and machine learning to solve problems that are beyond the reach of either working alone.

I became intrigued by crypto after learning that famous hedge fund managers Michael Novogratz and Adam Levinson from Fortress Investment Group had bought US$20 million of bitcoins in 2013. Today, that stash is worth close to US$200 million. In 2016, I created technology startups (such as Shentilium Technologies), but kept in touch with a colleague from Goldman Sachs named Mona El Isa, who would go on to create a crypto software provider called Melonport, and whom you'll meet at the end of this book.[8]

Perhaps in time to come, 2016 will be remembered as a watershed year for crypto, and less for the highly unlikely election of US President Donald Trump. Over and over again I would hear news about some new development in Bitcoin or the hundreds of new cryptos (and exchanges) seemingly popping up overnight. Many were appreciating in value, such as Ethereum; since I first heard of it, it's grown more than 40 times in value! And in fairness, Dimon has since changed his position on Bitcoin from hostility to neutrality.[9]

I experimented here and there with crypto, dipping my toe into the waters and learning what I could. Together with my crypto compatriot, Lee Hong, we had several meetings late at night teaching each other about blockchain technologies and cryptocurrency. We decided to go to DevCon 2 in Shanghai in

September 2016. I didn't make it in the end but Lee Hong did and befriended Loi Luu of Kyber Network.

My dual background in banking and tech caught the eyes of Kyber Network's development team, who approached me to advise on their new crypto exchange and help build it from the ground up by working alongside some of the best coders and engineers in the industry.

To that end, I spent several months immersed in what it truly takes to build and trade in crypto, especially in the days leading up to an *initial coin offering* (ICO). This is when a startup begins offering its own cryptocurrency to raise funds, potentially bypassing traditional forms of fundraising like offering shares or working with venture capitalists.

That means I know a promising information product when I see one, and in the case of crypto, I can actually show you how it works—and why it attracts the attention it does.

What You'll Learn

Think of me as a tour guide to the basics of crypto, giving you a knowledge base you can start out with as you decide whether or not to take the plunge into crypto trading. When our time together is done, you'll be able to:

- Follow a conversation or financial pages report about crypto and its value, and understand what it bodes for various cryptos such as Bitcoin, Ethereum, Dash, Litecoin and others.
- Set up an account for crypto buying, selling and mining, complete with your own *wallet* and set of transaction records, or blockchains.

- Understand the key issues that make crypto so alluring yet controversial (like any new technology), and its implications for investors, governments and banks.
- Tell what differentiates one crypto from another, in terms of their product positioning, accessibility, level of oversight and risk factor.
- See how and why half-truths and myths form so easily around crypto—and bust them with the truth.

Like any current financial instrument, crypto is here to stay, for better or worse. Even if there is indeed a crash (more on that later in the book) it's not going to wipe crypto out—only change the way it's dealt with.

Everyone is free to embrace it as the biggest revolution since Gutenberg's printing press; shrug and add some to their portfolios 'just in case'; dismiss it as a fraud; or completely ignore it in favour of 'safer' transactions and financial products. I can easily point you to even more intelligent, savvy and well-informed people who've taken each position. All I ask is that we decide from knowledge, not ignorance.

Of course, the usual boilerplate that this book doesn't constitute investment advice applies here. But I hope it'll equip you with what you need to make the most of it.

Whatever you decide, I wish you all the best in your financial journey. See you ahead!

Notes

[1] For more on the Dutch tulip craze and subsequent market crash in the 1630s, see: Andrew Beattie, "Market Crashes: The Tulip and Bulb Craze," *Investopedia*, (no date), at http://www.investopedia.com/features/crashes/crashes2.asp.

[2] Dimon quotes in: Hugh Son, Hannah Levitt and Brian Louis, "Jamie Dimon Slams Bitcoin as a 'Fraud,'" *Bloomberg*, 13 September 2017, at https://www.bloomberg.com/news/articles/2017-09-12/jpmorgan-s-ceo-says-he-d-fire-traders-who-bet-on-fraud-bitcoin. Draper quotes in: Laura Lorenzetti, "Venture capitalist Tim Draper wins government bitcoin auction," *Fortune*, 2 July 2014, at http://fortune. com/2014/07/02/venture-capitalist-draper-wins-bitcoin-auction.

[3] An example of the latter use: 'Cryptozoology' is the study of unknown or speculative organisms, like the Sasquatch, the Yeti, modern dinosaurs or the Loch Ness Monster.

[4] Rob Price, "Someone in 2010 bought 2 pizzas with 10,000 bitcoins — which today would be worth $20 million," *Business Insider UK*, 22 May 2017, at http://uk.businessinsider.com/bitcoin-pizza-day-passes-2000-20-million-2017-5/?IR=T. The Bitcoin community marks 22 May as Bitcoin Pizza Day.

[5] Kenneth Rapoza, "Goldman Sachs Caves: Bitcoin Is Money," Forbes, 10 January 2018, at https://www.forbes.com/sites/kenrapoza/2018/01/10/goldman-sachs-caves-bitcoin-is-money.

[6] "Frequently-asked Questions and Myths," *Bitcoin.org*, (no date), https://bitcoin.org/ en/faq.

[7] For the uninitiated, FX is foreign exchange trading—that is, where international currencies like the US dollar, the euro or the Chinese renminbi are traded.

[8] For more on Melonport and the services it provides, see: Melon, "What Is Melon?" *Medium. com*, 28 June 2017, at https://medium.com/melonport-blog/what-is-melon-f9bf41600b7e.

[9] Quoted in Omkar Godbole, "Jamie Dimon says he regrets calling Bitcoin a fraud," *Coindesk*, 10 January 2018, at https://www.coindesk.com/jamie-dimon-says-he-regrets-calling-bitcoin-a-fraud

CHAPTER 1

THE NEW GOLD MINING

> Is a man not entitled to the sweat of his brow? "No," says the man in Washington, "it belongs to the poor." "No," says the man in the Vatican, "it belongs to God." "No," says the man in Moscow, "it belongs to everyone." I rejected those answers; instead, I chose something different. I chose the impossible. I chose... Rapture.
>
> —*Bioshock (2007)*

In this chapter, you'll see:
- How and why the idea of crypto was birthed
- The processes and thinking that shaped its creation
- How Bitcoin (and most crypto) differs from cash, stocks and bonds

It is said that when then-California Governor Ronald Reagan visited a university in the 1960s, a student told him there was no way people like Reagan could understand young people. "You grew up in a different world," he said. "Today we have television, jet planes, space travel, nuclear energy, computers."

Reagan simply replied, "You're right. It's true that we didn't have those things when we were young. We invented them."[1]

Perhaps blockchain technology, and the cryptocurrencies and other applications that run on it, is our own generation's answer to Reagan. It might seem that crypto is entirely new, and indeed few people understand how money can be transacted safely without a single authority (like a bank) to make sure it's sent in the right amount, to the right person, at the right time.

As crypto took off, Satoshi Nakamoto himself would wonder how to explain it to others.

"Writing a description of this thing for general audiences is bloody hard," he once wrote. "There's nothing to relate it to."[2]

The best way to grasp the birth of crypto is to look into the past. It all starts with people trying to solve a defined problem— be it making fire, working out the speed of light or learning the structure of the DNA molecule.

The birth of the blockchain concept, and Nakamoto's rise to fame, can be compared (believe it or not) to the work being done on DNA in the 1950s. The iconic double helix was deduced by the work of biologists James Watson and Francis Crick, who noted in their famous 1953 paper, "A Structure for Deoxyribose Nucleic Acid": "It has not escaped our notice that the specific pairing we have postulated immediately suggests a possible pairing mechanism for the genetic material."[3]

That discovery won them the Nobel Prize. Notice that Watson and Crick were simply studying the DNA molecule to learn its structure—in hopes of unlocking the chemical basis of life, as one of many teams to do so. With their discovery came a promising new avenue, a means by which cells replicated their genetic material. Nearly all of what we know about genetic science stems from that single discovery, and the paper that followed.

Similarly, Nakamoto was working on a widespread, well-known problem among software engineers when he made the proposal that changed everything.

Cash Is King

Today, we send money to vendors and each other via bank transfer, PayPal or some other system that we take for granted. But we're using the winners of a competition held decades ago, when it was realised that financial transactions could indeed be made over the Internet. It may seem remote to us now, but the eighties were a time of great technological uncertainty as many of the things we take for granted today were still being figured out.

The idea of digital cash isn't new; it dates back to proposals made in the 1980s by mathematician David Chaum, whose paper "Untraceable Electronic Cash," outlined ecash, a system of anonymous cash transfers over the then-new Internet. He found partners in cryptography (that is, the science of encoding information so it can only be seen by its intended recipients) and started his own company, DigiCash, in an attempt to commercialise the idea.

"At this moment in history," observes finance writer Dominic Frisby, "credit cards were still considered unsafe and insecure. It was not clear who was going to win the battle to control internet payments."[4]

Of course, no prizes for guessing which system won out in the end. Despite much interest from partners like Microsoft (which wanted to integrate ecash into Windows 95) and major banks such as ING, Chaum insisted on holding out for more money—refusing to sign lucrative deals that might have sealed his product as a pioneer of electronic cash transfer. In the end, his backers lost interest and the offers dried up as they sought a less obstinate partner. Credit cards won that battle, and in 1999 Digicash went out of business entirely.

Other models would be tried. Frisby cites e-gold, which allowed users to buy physical gold using accounts on its website, and sell portions of it to others. Its pioneering firm grew into a success story from its founding in 1996, until its widespread use by criminals led to the FBI taking an interest in the late 2000s. "It fell victim to hacking, fraud and identity theft [...] By 2009, it had been shut down. Its founders faced all sorts of legal calamities—and are still dealing with the fall-out."[5]

Perhaps, Frisby notes, this is one reason why Nakamoto remains completely anonymous. If he were conclusively identified, it would make Bitcoin far more susceptible to regulation, and therefore much less empowering than he envisioned it to be.

Nakamoto definitely had the fates of ecash and e-gold on his mind when he wrote:

> A lot of people automatically dismiss e-currency as a lost cause because of all the companies that failed since the 1990s. I hope it's obvious it was only the centrally controlled nature of those systems that doomed them. I think this is the first time we're trying a decentralised, non-trust-based system.[6]

Because the past attempts at digital cash were set up by established companies with names, faces and identities to them, they were tied entirely to the people that produced them. In other words, they had a central point of failure—something Bitcoin, with its peer-to-peer, networked nature doesn't have. Because no one can be said to administer Bitcoin, there's no single entity whose trouble will spell the end.

Double-Spending

Why are banks still needed when you transact digitally? Because their authority is needed to verify that you haven't spent money you don't (or no longer) have.

You see, electronic payments have a vulnerability that physical ones don't, namely the problem of *double-spending*—the possibility that a packet of data representing a given transaction is sent, but a copy kept by the sender so they appear not to have sent anything. When money is sent in the form of electronic data, it's far easier to duplicate, as it's simply a matter of copying and pasting code. Physical currency by definition is more difficult to fake, needing expensive counterfeiting equipment to defeat the measures that mints have put into place.[7] Also, a genuine coin or note can only exist in one place at a time. Once you've spent it, it's gone from your possession.

Besides processing the payment, computers belonging to your issuing bank need to verify that you're you and that you actually have the money you're sending. After you've sent it, they must confirm that it's no longer in your possession. Those are the tests your transaction needs to pass before you can see that comforting green tick on the screen.

Investopedia outlines the problem as follows:

Double-spending is a problem unique to digital currencies because digital information can be reproduced relatively easily. Physical currencies do not have this issue because they cannot be easily replicated, and the parties involved in a transaction can immediately verify the bona fides of the physical currency. With digital currency, there is a risk that the holder could make a copy of the digital token and send it to a merchant or another party while retaining the original.[8]

A simpler explanation is offered by Ofir Beigel of 99Bitcoins.com. Suppose a sender has only one bitcoin. He makes a transaction sending that bitcoin to recipient A, sending it into a pool of unconfirmed transactions. Before Transaction A can be confirmed, the sender makes another one-bitcoin transaction, sending it to recipient B.

Now both transactions are in the pool, awaiting confirmation by the network. The transaction that gets confirmed first is treated as final, and the second is discarded. But what if the confirmation process for the two happened simultaneously? "Both transactions will show that I have the money needed," Beigel points out. In other words, the same bitcoin (or dollar) can be spent twice![9]

I'll say more about how Nakamoto dealt with this problem in the next chapter. Traditionally, the problem of double-spending has been solved through financial institutions (which Nakamoto called '*mints*') setting their services up as intermediaries that verify that each party in the transaction is who they say they are, and that all monies successfully sent are received in good order.

But there is one very, very serious flaw with this approach: That you have to entrust your money with a financial authority, and as history has shown, it leaves that money vulnerable to poor risk management on their part.

When They Let You Down

Nakamoto and his fellow coders were deeply sceptical of the central control wielded by said trusted authorities—and the possibility that they were taking unwarranted risks with money they did not own. The concept of Bitcoin grew out of the 2008 financial crisis, a time when many people lost faith in banks and central authorities.

As 'Prypto', the author of *Bitcoin for Dummies*, tells it:

As the global financial system teetered on the brink of collapse, many central banks engaged in quantitative easing—or in simple terms, turned on the printing presses. Central banks flooded the markets with liquidity and slashed interest rates to near zero in order to prevent a repeat of the Great Depression of the 1930s.

The effect of this was large-scale fluctuations in fiat currencies and what has since been termed currency wars—a race to competitively devalue so that an economy can become more viable simply by its goods and services being cheaper than those of its neighbors and global competitors.[10]

The result? Currencies lost value as more of it got printed, and governments were forced to pay billions of taxpayer dollars to save failing banks. The entire financial market took many terrible shocks that are still being felt today, nearly a decade on. It became suspected by many that central bankers:

> ... were taking many economies into the unknown and were prepared to devalue their fiat currencies at will just to keep the wheels turning. In doing so, they bailed out the very same institutions and bankers whose reckless behavior had brought about this crisis in the first place.[11]

To Nakamoto, currency control was too critical to be left completely to bankers and financial institutions. By believing that financial institutions knew better and entrusting such authority to them, entire populations (and their governments) were setting themselves up for failure. "The root problem with conventional currency is all the trust that's required to make it work," he told forum users at the P2P Foundation. "The central bank must be trusted not to debase the currency, but the history of fiat currencies is full of breaches of that trust."[12]

Rather, he believed that a secure, tamper-proof payment system that bypassed the need for central verification (while replicating the ability of mints to handle transactions) was the solution. He realised that the key was not to trust anyone or anything but the sheer power of industrial-grade encryption and the ability to break it.

Nakamoto's plan would rest on *decentralisation*, or breaking up the load of creating, decrypting and distributing the money into smaller processes performed by different entities. To do this, he would have to solve four key problems:

- How can identities be verified in a way satisfactory to both parties?
- How can everyone agree on what transactions have been made, and when?
- How can everyone be sure that they have the latest information?
- How can the records, once set, be protected from being tampered with?

We don't know if Nakamoto actually set out to create a new currency with the same agreed-on worth as others, but that was the natural direction his discovery took him to. The result was his 2008 white paper "Bitcoin: A Peer-to-Peer Electronic Cash System,"[13] which he first published to the cryptography mailing list of metzdowd.com. Its architecture was simple in its construction, and I'll go through the basics of Nakamoto's paper and Bitcoin, the first cryptocurrency, in the next chapter.

Bitcoin's birthday is regarded to be 3 January 2009, when Nakamoto released the first-ever 'block' of Bitcoin, a package of 50 coins known to this day as the Genesis Block. At the same time, he released the full source code of the Bitcoin software on open-source distribution site SourceForge—all 31,000 lines of it. The first recipient of bitcoins was one of Nakamoto's closest collaborators, a programmer named Harold 'Hal' Finney. (Sadly, Finney died in 2014 of motor neurone disease; if he knew who Nakamoto really was, he has taken the secret to his grave.)

It's possible, even likely, that Nakamoto is actually an entire development team hiding behind a single pseudonym. This is the conclusion reached by several researchers who have studied Bitcoin's source code, including cybersecurity pioneer Dan Kaminsky, who attacked it in every way he knew—only to give up when the code resisted every attempt.

And thus the new currency was born. A cash exchange system not issued by a central bank, and with records maintained by computers around the world, not a single entry point where hackers could enter and steal. Once Bitcoin came online, it was indestructible from any single point; no government, hacker or power can shut Bitcoin down, because as long as even one node is active, Bitcoin will continue to exist.

Crypto Today

Just as genetic science in the post-double helix world exploded, so did financial markets when the true implications of Nakamoto's work emerged. I'll share more about why Bitcoin is so controversial, but the result has been the proliferation of new forms of electronic currency (Bitcoin alternatives, or *altcoins*) that claim to do what Bitcoin does, or better. Some even have the backing of the very same banks that Nakamoto worked to cut down to size.

At the very least, you'll be hard-pressed to find a modern bank that doesn't take the idea of crypto very, very seriously, to the extent of publishing about it, partnering with crypto startups or introducing laws to protect people from scams and crashes. As the fintech chief of Singapore's Monetary Authority, Sopnendu Mohanty, has said: "We know exactly when to intervene, based on the market size and the demand and transaction volume, and we will come in at the right time. So, I'm not overly worried about getting to some large financial system crisis."[14]

Will the Real Satoshi Nakamoto Please Stand Up?

What has become of Nakamoto himself? He quietly handed over his websites and Bitcoin programming assets, then vanished from the community in 2010, citing his move to "other projects".

Whoever Nakamoto really is, he (or they) would never assume the identity again. However, there is no guarantee that he will not resurface or be unmasked—whether by his own hand or some brilliant detective work—at some point in the future.[15]

The secrecy is not for want of trying, and when the value of Bitcoin increased sharply over the years, journalists took great pains to try to expose him.

None have succeeded. A recent rumour has it, however, that he may be working with blockchain startup Ethereum.

Whether Nakamoto truly succeeded in eroding the power of central banking and mint-verified payment remains to be seen. What he did do was kick off an entirely new market worth hundreds of billions of dollars that did not even exist a decade ago. You'll find crypto used by everyone from well-known businesses to criminals on the Dark Web, and thousands of merchants accept payment in Bitcoin and other cryptos—wherever it is allowed as legal tender.

What's the Big Deal, Anyway?

The birth of Bitcoin and the entire cryptocurrency movement is ushering in a new era of technological independence, with people participating in it as they choose—rather than being hand-held, or arm-twisted, into accepting terms and conditions that may not be to their liking. One way of thinking about it is considering that crypto and blockchains are to Uber or Grab as banks are to traditional taxi and car rental firms.

In both cases, the former provides convenience and participation at each person's own discretion, though one must necessarily give up some control, safety and a formal accountability structure. Instead, you're the sole decision-maker of what happens to your crypto—though what you learn in this book and from the community will be a great help in storing, investing and using it.

A look at the market shows how popular Bitcoin has become. Since 2011, Bitcoin's value has shot up thousands of times, and is steadily increasing to this day. This is a credit not just to Bitcoin, but the model itself; altcoin Ethereum's value has been rocketing up since mid-2016.

This freedom must be responsibly used, though—because once you lose access to your crypto or make a transaction you later regret, there's no way to reverse it, short of the recipient willingly sending it back to you. In this book, I'll share not only the processes, but the thought patterns you must bring to the party so as to handle crypto safely.

Just turn the page to get started.

Your New Blocks

- Bitcoin was conceptualised as a means of electronic cash transfer which eliminated the need to trust any centralised entity or institution.
- Double-spending is a problem unique to electronic cash transfer; because the money exists only as computer code, there must be a way to prevent a single dollar from being copied and spent over and over again.
- The double-spending problem in electronic cash transfer was traditionally solved by a trusted party (such as a bank) declaring the transaction complete; Bitcoin achieves this by decentralising the process and having multiple Internet-connected computers compete to do so.
- Owners are the sole decision-makers of what happens to their cryptocurrencies—there is no authority over the system itself.
- Despite its anonymous origin, Bitcoin has now become a commodity worth millions of dollars in its own right.

Notes

[1] Quoted in Ronald Reagan, "Remarks and a Question-and-Answer Session With Senior Citizens in Los Angeles, California," *UCSB American Presidency Project*, 6 July 1982, at http://www.presidency.ucsb.edu/ws/?pid=42708.

[2] Satoshi Nakamoto, post in "Slashdot Submission for 1.0," 5 July 2010, Bitcoin forum, at https://bitcointalk.org/index.php?topic=234.msg1976#msg1976.

[3] The full paper is available at https://www.nature.com/nature/dna50/watsoncrick.pdf.

[4] Dominic Frisby, *Bitcoin, The Future of Money?* (Marylebone, London, UK: Unbound, 2014), "The evolution of digital cash – and the monies that failed".

[5] Ibid.

[6] Satoshi Nakamoto, forum post on 15 February 2009, at http://p2pfoundation.ning.com/ forum/topics/bitcoin-open-source?commentId=2003008%3AComment%3A9493.

[7] For example, many countries print banknotes with holographic images, unique serial numbers and markings that only show up under ultraviolet light. The equipment needed to do so is so specialised and expensive as to be (it is hoped) beyond the reach of counterfeiters.

[8] "Double Spending," *Investopedia*, (no date), at http://www.investopedia.com/terms/d/ doublespending.asp.

[9] Ofir Beigel, "What Is Double-Spending?" *99Bitcoins.com*, 29 April 2014, at https://99bitcoins.com/double-spending.

[10] Prypto, "The Origin of Bitcoin," *Dummies.com*, (no date), at http://www.dummies.com/ software/other-software/the-origin-of-bitcoin.

[11] Ibid.

[12] Satoshi Nakamoto, "Bitcoin open source implementation of P2P currency," *P2P Foundation*, 11 February 2009, at http://p2pfoundation.ning.com/forum/topics/bitcoin-open-source.

[13] The entire paper is available at the Bitcoin Foundation's website, at www.bitcoin.org/ bitcoin.pdf.

[14] Lua Jiamin and Lin Xueling, "Bitcoin won't end in a Lehman Brothers-like crash, says MAS fintech chief," *CAN Insider*, 25 January 2018, at https://www.channelnewsasia.com/news/ cnainsider/bitcoin-cryptocurrency-lehman-financial-crash-risk-mas-fintech-9893862.

[15] The sole exception came in March 2014, when a Japanese-American engineer coincidentally named Dorian Satoshi Nakamoto was fingered by *Newsweek* as being the Nakamoto who created Bitcoin. But the journalist had gotten it entirely wrong; Dorian Nakamoto had never even heard of Bitcoin and vehemently denied it. In the media frenzy that followed, the P2P Foundation account of Bitcoin's creator briefly broke a four-year silence with a single forum post. It simply read, "I am not Dorian Nakamoto."

CHAPTER 2

CRYPTO 101:
HOW CRYPTO AND BLOCKCHAINS WORK

But I found myself in the midst of a strange people, who, seeing me come from the clouds, thought I was a great Wizard.

—L Frank Baum, *The Wonderful Wizard of Oz*

In this chapter, you'll see:

- The basic mechanics behind crypto, blockchains and mining
- What makes them unbreakable in the real world
- Where crypto gets its monetary value

The titular Wizard of Oz is supposedly a being of great magical power. Our suspicions are raised, however, when he sends Dorothy and her companions to take out the Wicked Witch of the West. Why, we wonder, does he not do it himself?

In the end, the Wizard is revealed for who he really is—an ordinary man with just enough engineering skill to fool all of them. His powers come from science, not wizardry.

Something like that happens when we open up crypto and learn what makes it tick. It's certainly true that blockchains are a new invention, but as we've seen the technological and social foundation of its rise has been in place as early as the 1990s.

Fortunately for us, Bitcoin's architecture is open-source, available for anyone to see, modify and re-distribute; this Wizard isn't hiding from us, but has thrown back the curtain from the very beginning.[1] Anyone with the ability and funding can very easily replicate or modify the code, and create their own cryptocurrency.

(Indeed, the altcoin known as Dogecoin was created as a joke to show how easily saturated the market could become. Somehow, serious investors didn't see it that way. By June 2017, Dogecoin was a successful method of tipping for services, and had a total value of US$340 million.)

I'm going to use the example of Bitcoin, but the broad principles apply to any cryptocurrency out there. After all, as BlockGeeks points out:

If you take away all the noise around cryptocurrencies and reduce it to a simple definition, you find it to be just limited entries in a database no one can change without fulfilling specific conditions. This may seem ordinary, but, believe it or not: this is exactly how you can define a currency.

Take the money on your bank account: What is it more than entries in a database that can only be changed under specific conditions? You can even take physical coins and notes: What are they else than limited entries in a public physical database that can only be changed if you match the condition than you physically own the coins and notes? Money is all about a verified entry in some kind of database of accounts, balances, and transactions.[2]

Let There Be Coin

Bitcoin began as a white paper published to a popular website's cryptography forums in the ancient era that we now know as 2008. In its opening abstract, Nakamoto summarised the basic concept of his new value-storage system, detailing how it would work and why it was needed.

It's a single paragraph, but it's a clear, succinct description of how Bitcoin works. To make explanation easier, I've broken it down into six parts:

1. A purely peer-to-peer version of electronic cash would allow online payments to be sent directly from one party to another without going through a financial institution.
2. Digital signatures provide part of the solution, but the main benefits are lost if a trusted third party is still required to prevent double-spending. We propose a solution to the double-spending problem using a peer-to-peer network.
3. The network timestamps transactions by hashing them into an ongoing chain of hash-based proof-of-work, forming a record that cannot be changed without redoing the proof-of-work.
4. The longest chain not only serves as proof of the sequence of events witnessed, but proof that it came from the largest pool of CPU power.

5. As long as a majority of CPU power is controlled by nodes that are not cooperating to attack the network, they'll generate the longest chain and outpace attackers.

6. The network itself requires minimal structure. Messages are broadcast on a best effort basis, and nodes can leave and rejoin the network at will, accepting the longest proof-of-work chain as proof of what happened while they were gone.

Each statement is full of implications, so let's go through the abstract one part at a time. I've kept the language as simple and jargon-free as possible, although some is unavoidable.

Part 1: Why decentralised peer-to-peer (P2P) networks work better for sending money from one party to another

Note that Nakamoto doesn't even call his idea a new currency, or even a means of storing money at this point. It's merely a way to verify payments that sidesteps the need for a central authority.

Just as a file can be shared via a P2P connection, a transaction can be made simply by creating a record that Nate has sent Manash X dollars.

Indeed, this is the very definition of money—some arbitrary, easily-available item both parties agree has value takes the place of barter trading. Earlier, if rice-farmer Nate needed to trade with corn-farmer Manash, they were out of luck if either party had no need of both crops. Money fills this gap by establishing an amount each product is worth, and providing an easy way of exchanging that amount. In the case of cash notes, that amount is represented through slips of paper with the government-assigned value printed on them.

P2P networks have been around since the beginning of the Internet, and it can be argued that the World Wide Web itself began as one. A P2P network is simply an arrangement of computers set up for sharing files and services. You might even have one in your office, in the form of a shared drive for storing files any of your colleagues can access and update, or a connected printer.

How P2P Works

How is a P2P system different from other system setups? Margaret Rouse writes on techtarget.com:

> [P2P is] a decentralised communications model in which each party has the same capabilities and either party can initiate a communication session. Unlike the client/server model, in which the client makes a service request and the server fulfills the request, the P2P network model allows each node to function as both a client and server.[3]

This means there is no distinction between service provider and client, and every connected node is treated as an equal, or 'peer'. Anyone can send or carry out a service request, and it is this flexibility that allows P2P to transact payments reliably. What Nakamoto proposes is the fact that a financial institution such as a bank or broker need not even be part of the picture, not even for the largest transactions.

We're used to having our banks and stores confirm charges like credit card payments and automated billing through receipts. But such trust has a darker side, as we have seen in big banks' abuse of their power to take unwarranted risks, dooming unsuspecting customers in the process. Instead, Nakamoto's method would use a secure P2P system to completely remove trust from the picture, and replicate the verification systems set up by those institutions.

Implied here is the need not to use any existing currency, because it would be entirely dependent on government action to maintain its value.

Part 2 : Why existing tech doesn't both remove the need for trust and solve the problem of double-spending

Nakamoto acknowledges a partial solution to the verification problem described in **part 1**—that of digital signatures.

A digital signature works by encrypting something sent from one person to another. The sender's computer 'signs' a transaction with a public key *derived* from his private key when it is sent. A copy of the public key is sent along with the document, and this public key functions as proof that the document did indeed come from the sender. The recipient is then able to open the document using the public key; anyone who intercepts the document halfway is unlikely to possess the key and tamper with the message.

However, digital signatures on their own don't solve the problem of double-spending. This is an issue unique to electronic money transfers because digital data can be so easily copied.

We've seen what double-spending is, and why it's such a problem—and a big part of the reason why banks continue to be trusted.

Nakamoto proposed that a P2P network could solve this problem through 'chains' of records, with each new link in the chain specially encrypted so as to sync with the link before it, in the same way a new piece on a jigsaw puzzle snaps into place. A transaction would be decrypted, checked and authorised (or discarded) before being added to the chain—the one checked using more computing power would be done faster and hence be the winner.

The record of successful transactions is then finalised and added as a new entry (or 'block') to a publicly available ledger, which we know today as a blockchain.

A blockchain, then, is simply the public record of all transactions made, which is regularly synchronised among all the members of the network. In the case of Bitcoin, it only records that Address A has sent X bitcoins to Address B—plus a means of connecting the 'block' containing that transaction to the past blocks in the chain, which Nakamoto explores in **part 3**.

Besides this, each address is a meaningless string of letters and numbers. There is no indication in the chain itself about the real-world people or organisations using the addresses.

Part 3: How security via a cryptographic algorithm removes the need to trust any one party with transaction information

Here, Nakamoto gets technical. He explains **part 2**'s idea of how a P2P network can authorise transactions through encrypting them, but not in the same way as digital signatures.

This is where we enter the world of encryption. Every new block is time-stamped and encoded via a special cypher, and the result is a 'fingerprint' of the original data known as a *hash*.

Hashes for the Math-Minded

Alexey Malanov, a researcher at Internet security firm Kaspersky Lab, explains how hashes work like this:

Let's create a numeric representation of "Hello". Here's one way to do that: Let each letter be associated with a sequential number (i.e., a=1, b=2, z=26), so Hello would read 8*5*12*12*15.

Multiply the numbers to get 86400. That's how we get the simplest hash.

After I have sent a primary message to my friend, I send the hash so that they can check whether the received message matches the intended one.

Now, what if the message was altered on its way, and now it reads "Hallo"? Well, that would change its hash: 8*1*12*12*15=17280. My friend would expect to get 86400, so when they get 17280, the difference would alert us both that something went wrong.[4]

In most secure applications such as email, hashes are sent along with each message invisibly to the sender.

Hashes are designed not to betray any information about the text they encrypt, and change drastically if even a single parameter in the source file is tweaked—as we saw in the example above.

Of course, actual hashes are far more complex than this but they all use the same principle of ensuring that data is protected from corruption when it is transmitted, whether by accident or design—through comparison of the hashes in the received and sent documents.

In Bitcoin's case, the mathematical ability to decrypt the hash counts as Nakamoto's proof-of-work. This term refers to a piece of data that is computationally extremely difficult to produce, but easy for others to verify. The various nodes use their computing power competitively, solving the hash in the quickest time possible, and the 'winner', having the proof-of-work, gets the right to add a new block to the chain.

"Proof-of-work has the nice property that it can be relayed through untrusted middlemen," Nakamoto observed. "We don't have to worry about a chain of custody of communication. It doesn't matter who tells you a longest chain, the proof-of-work speaks for itself."[5] In other words, there's nothing to trust. The mere fact that the cypher has been broken is enough.

What kind of mathematical problems are involved? The actual hash that Bitcoin uses is beyond the scope of this book, but here's a simpler example.

An actual cypher called RSA uses the fact that it's very easy to multiply two very large prime numbers together to produce a composite number; any calculator can do this. But given the composite number, it's extremely difficult even for a supercomputer to reproduce the two prime numbers (that is, numbers divisible only by themselves and 1, such as 2, 3, 5, 7 and so on) that produced it.

Yet once the correct answer is arrived at, it's simple to check against the original product—this can be done simply by multiplying the two primes together. Adrian Berry says it best in his book *Galileo and the Dolphins*: "It is easy to turn a pig into pork sausages, but very difficult to turn pork sausages back into a pig."

When the first miner to solve the hash does so, it's assumed that more computing power was put into doing this, and the computer that solved it gets the right to add to the blockchain. In the case of Bitcoin, the miner receives a block reward. This is 12.5 bitcoins as of 2018, and halves every four years. Also included are the transaction fees of any transactions the miner decides to verify and include in the block. (I say more about mining later on in this chapter.)

Once this is done, the blockchain is theoretically immutable; a change in any block to show that Party X did not spend any bitcoins would be impossible without changing every subsequent block. That would require "redoing the proof-of-work" many times over—a task that needs more computing power and time than is, or ever will be, available.

This is how verified transactions can be made without the need for any central authority. On the other hand, this also means there is no way to reverse a fraudulent or unwanted transaction.

It's both a strength and a weakness, as we'll see.

Part 4: How we know our transaction information will always be accurate and up-to-date

With this system in place, Nakamoto points out that there'll never be any doubt that the publicly-available ledger will always be up-to-date, as surely as if your bank had pronounced it to be so. Because the computer that solves the most hashes will have the longest record, it can be safely assumed that it has the new 'master' copy of the new block. Every place where the blockchain is stored will be updated accordingly; everyone now has an up-to-date record, and the race begins again.

Imagine I offered you a bottle of fine wine at a premium price, say $1,000 a bottle. I justify the price by insisting it's been aged 40 years at a chateau in the South of France. Of course, the question is, how do you know whether this bottle is indeed worth the price I say it is? How can you verify that my claim is accurate?

I've just shown precisely the problem that blockchains solve. Without it, you'll just have to take my word for it—or consult a detailed ledger that breaks down exactly when the wine was produced, how long it's been aged and how far it's travelled. No one's got time for that ... and how do you know the ledger hasn't been tampered with? How do you know the wine itself isn't some cheap imitation from the corner store?

The answer lies in the computing power needed to add each new entry to the ledger of movement. Because the sole surviving record is by definition the one written down and backed up with more computing power, it can't have been tampered with after the fact.

Plus the wine is physically where the blockchain's latest entry says it will be—which with the blockchain, is all the proof you need that the wine did indeed originate and travel where it says it did.

Part 5: Why a decentralised network can't be easily altered, providing security from tampering

This is actually easier to understand than it sounds, and the benefits of decentralisation were understood even in antiquity. In *The Prince*, his classical work of statecraft and realpolitik, the fourteenth-century Italian diplomat Niccolo Machiavelli pointed out the key difference between centralised and decentralised authority:

> The whole of Turkey is governed by one ruler, or sultan. Everyone serves him. He divides his realm into provinces, or *sanjaks*, and sends administrators to run them, appointing and dismissing them as he sees fit.
>
> The King of France, on the other hand, is surrounded by any number of barons whose rights date back to ancient times and who are acknowledged and loved by their subjects. Each baron has specific privileges which a king can only take away at his peril. Looking at these two kinds of states, it's clear that Turkey is hard to conquer but once conquered very easy to hold. France on the other hand will be somewhat easier to conquer but very hard to hold.[6]

I'm sure the parallel becomes clear—central banking and trusted verification is like Turkey, where "there are no barons to invite you in" and any attacker will face a united foe that stands against them in the name of the Sultan. "Since subjects are the king's servants and indebted to him it's hard to corrupt them, and even assuming you do manage to bribe someone he's not likely to be much help," Machiavelli wrote. But once that foe has been defeated and the Sultan replaced, the attacker's gains are much easier to keep.

On the other hand, a P2P network is like France in Machiavelli's time. There might be a nominal king (and Bitcoin doesn't even have that), but real power lies in the hands of its barons—in the case of a P2P network like Bitcoin, those 'barons' are individual users like you and me. An outside force might be able to gain the support of one or two barons and begin to influence things, but were it to take over the entire country, it would have a very difficult time holding on to it. As Machiavelli explains:

> But afterwards you're going to have all kinds of problems holding on to what you've won, problems with the people who fought on your side and problems with those who fought against you and lost.[7]

Decentralisation has a critical strength in that you cannot simply take over a network that has no centre; like with France and its territories, it must be captured node by node, then held only at great cost.

Nakamoto assures his readers that his method will, by setting up competition for the right to authorise transactions, make it extremely difficult for the network to be taken over by any one party. In part 5, he reveals the only way the blockchain can be compromised—if someone were able to obtain more than half of the network's entire computing power, they could authorise any transaction they wanted, because they would solve every hash faster than anyone else and produce the sole 'approved' version of every block from there on out.

However, taking over half the computers involved in writing the blockchain (which, remember, comprises every miner of Bitcoin there has ever been) would be impossible—financially, logistically and economically—even for the most determined of attackers. It's the scale of such a task that makes the structure of Bitcoin itself so secure.

Of course, there are always exceptions, which we'll tackle in a later chapter.

Part 6: Why participation is voluntary and the network needs little formal structure

Because all new additions to the chains can be assumed to have the most computing power behind them, and therefore can be regarded as trustworthy, it follows that the longest chain must be the latest, correct one. In other words, a participant can be assured that the longest chain will contain all the transaction information he or she missed. Therefore, nodes (and by extension, Bitcoin users) can enter or leave the network at their discretion.

The result is that the Bitcoin network itself would need few 'authorities' around, with the blockchains providing a self-correcting mechanism. In effect, Nakamoto's proposal would replace the need to trust an outside authority with the challenge of cracking a fiendishly difficult code.

Therefore, no one polices Bitcoin. Policies are proposed by a development team called Bitcoin Core—but even they need a large majority buy-in from miners and users, creating a truly democratic currency run by its users, not government fiat. Whether this experiment succeeds, of course, it is too early to tell.

Bitcoin is, in effect, a system of stored value that gets that value from being mined, and is stored on an anonymous ledger that everyone can see... but no one can trace to a real-world identity, or corrupt without going to great cost to do so.

What's Mining, Anyway?

In January 1848, a California sawmill operator named James W Marshall claimed to have found gold deposits at Sutter's Mill, where he worked in Coloma, California. Before long, thousands of prospectors had descended on the site, and the mill itself failed as every able-bodied man went prospecting himself! It was one of the greatest mass migrations in history, with the largest waves arriving in 1849. Marshall himself would continue the search, only to die in 1885 without ever finding a sizeable haul.

However, very few of the millions of forty-niners ever struck it rich, with many dying on the hazardous journey across oceans, mountains and deserts. These were the days before the Panama Canal, making the sea passage from the North American East to West Coast a hazardous, months-long journey down and around the tip of South America.

But there was a crucial side effect. Entire industries grew to support them, turning California itself into one of the most economically prosperous territories and drawing it into the fold of the growing United States. The largest cities there, particularly

San Francisco, owe their growth from ghost towns to the vast demands of the migrants for shipping, supplies and living necessities. (San Francisco's American football team is named the 49ers in their honour.)

In effect, the best way to become rich was to sell to prospectors, not become one yourself! But the Gold Rush is merely one example of a valuable commodity's power to change fortunes. From the veritable Bitcoin mining industry that has sprung up practically overnight, it's possible that we're seeing a new, safer and potentially more rewarding age of gold-rushing.

In Bitcoin parlance, new blocks are added to the chain through the work of *miners*, people who run its mining software on their computers; these machines are therefore known as mining rigs. The reason why it's called mining is because in the same way gold and precious metals are dug out of the earth at great cost and risk, new bitcoins must be obtained from the system through the computing power of those rigs.

The Bitcoin network relies on miners to create new blocks and add them to Bitcoin's public blockchain—each block containing the record of all successful transactions. For their hard work, they are rewarded with a transaction fee set by the payer, as well as new bitcoins from the system.

Like with gold, silver and precious metals, Bitcoin derives its value from both its scarcity and utility. Despite being nothing more than a set of encrypted files, crypto must still follow the laws of economics to be worth anything. For instance, if the market were flooded with anything, such that supply always met demand, its price would crash. If gold became as common as graphite, there'd be no need to keep Fort Knox open! Real-world mining is difficult, dangerous work, and once in a while we read of miners being trapped deep underground or killed in accidents. But that's part of the difficulty, and the reason for the minerals' value.

Bitcoin prevents over-supply through making mining an intentionally difficult, time- and energy-consuming process, and setting the limit at 21 million bitcoins. As of this writing, about 80% has been mined.

In crypto-mining, the scarcity comes from Nakamoto's cyphers (or *hashes*). Mining crypto is simply using your hardware's computing power to solve those hashes over the Internet; how fast this is done is measured by the machine's *hash rate*. When you read of hardware being used to mine crypto, this is the feature most prominently shown.

I'm not going to compare crypto-mining to the experience of the forty-niners, as the worst physical danger they face is starting a fire from all the heat their farms generate. Mining can be rewarding, and with Bitcoin worth so much as we speak, there is intense competition to get the next block into circulation.

In the same way that the difficulty of gold mining controls its value and the rate at which it enters the market, cryptos adjust their mining protocols accordingly depending on the number of miners at work. Bitcoin relies on the steady creation of a new block every 10 minutes, and if difficulty remained constant, more miners would solve the hash in less and less time, flooding the market with valueless bitcoins. Instead, Bitcoin's software increases the difficulty of solving the hash the more miners enter the network so that the time taken for block addition will always be 10 minutes. If the world's miners are cracking it in less time, either by contributing more processing power or growing in number, it gets harder. If it's being done slower through less processing power or fewer miners, it gets easier.[8]

The reward for mining a block stands at 12.5 bitcoins, but this reward is halved every four years (or every 210,000 blocks) in a set process known as Bitcoin halving. (It was 25 bitcoins until July 2016, and the next halving will be in May 2020.) This rewards early adopters and limits the ability of Bitcoin to inflate.

Because one bitcoin is worth thousands of dollars, even a share in a mining operation has the potential to be very lucrative—if the price of a single bitcoin is say, US$10,000, the winning miner receives a payout effectively worth $125,000. An adopter who begins mining only after the 2020 halving, however, will only receive 6.25 bitcoins should he win the race. Assuming one bitcoin is still worth $10,000, he will only net $62,500.

This will be the case until all its 21 million units have been put into the market, and after this point, miners will receive their income from verifying transactions and adding them to blocks to be officially recognised in Bitcoin's history. If these rules remain in effect, the last bitcoin will be mined sometime around the year 2140.

Can I Mine at Home?

Just as metal miners contribute manpower and equipment to the cause, crypto-miners give computer processing hardware. As people realised that more computing power would increase their chances of creating new blocks, they realised the solution was to organise and pool their hardware.

In theory, anyone with an Internet connection can download and install the software needed, and begin using their computer as a mining rig. However, because the single most important factor is pure processing power, the lion's share of mining is done by such *mining farms*—organisations that buy mining hardware in bulk and install it in large rooms purposely set up near power plants, preferably in cooler climates to reduce the cost of cooling. The raw computing power is supplied by chips known as Application-Specific Integrated Circuits (ASICs), and investors 'chip in' by paying a portion of the power bills and the costs of the hardware needed, in return for a cut of any payouts.

Of course, there are significant costs—not least the sheer amount of electrical power needed to run all that. In effect, miners hope to profit by obtaining enough blocks such that they earn more than they spend on their power bills. More computing power means they spend more money on hardware, electricity and cooling, but gain a higher chance of getting the reward.

Unfortunately, this means that the race to mine new bitcoins has become (in my view) completely inaccessible to home miners, as the only way to beat a mining farm is to start a bigger one. If you must mine, consider one of the altcoins specially set up to be more easily mined by home users, such as Ether or Bitcoin Gold.

How Transactions Work:
Or, Why You Can't Send Crypto You Don't Have
That's not all miners do; they play a crucial role in verifying the thousands of transactions that occur each hour, ensuring

that people only spend bitcoins they actually own and solving the double-spending problem, as outlined in parts 2 and 3 of Nakamoto's abstract. When all 21 million bitcoins have been mined, mining revenue will only come from verifying transactions. As a reward for including the transaction in the new block, the miner receives a *transaction fee* set by the payer.

"Since Bitcoin is peer-to-peer and there is no central authority to control it, [everyone] can send any kind of transaction to the network, whether or not it is valid," writes Steven Roose on StackExchange.com's Bitcoin forum. "You could simply send a transaction that sends someone else's coins to yourself."[9]

However, he notes that mining removes the ability of individual users to do this and succeed. While such a transaction might indeed get sent, a miner trying to authorise that transaction by loading it into a block would quickly find it is invalid when they try to upload it to the network and join it to the existing blockchain.

In short, every transaction in that miner's block needs to be valid (in miner parlance, a 'beautiful' block) before it can officially be considered part of Bitcoin's history. A block containing an invalid transaction would be very unlikely to succeed in being placed, and once part of the chain, a block can no longer be tampered with to reverse the transactions it contains.

And because only valid blocks get added, the 'correct' chain used by all parties is therefore the one with the most successful transactions—that is, the longest. It is therefore in every miner's self-interest to only load valid transactions into their blocks.

In short, Nakamoto's achievement wasn't simply pulling a new financial product out of thin air. It was decentralising and making 'trustless', what originally needed a trusted, central authority to verify, creating a network of participation all over the world, and ushering in a new way of thinking about money transfers.

Your New Block

- Bitcoin is a peer-to-peer cash transfer system and value store that exists only on the Internet; ownership is determined by a ledger of transactions from one anonymous address to another, known as a blockchain.
- The blockchain can only be added to when a computer user (known as a *miner*) uses a mining rig to break the encryption surrounding the new transaction or store of bitcoins, by using CPU power to solve mathematical problems of controlled difficulty. Miners around the world compete to do this first.
- The first miner to do so is assumed to have invested the most computing power to do so; its version of the resulting blockchain is thus the 'correct' one, and every member of the network updates its copy of the chain accordingly.
- Bitcoin is decentralised, and the only way an attacker can authorise fraudulent transactions is for it to possess more than half the total computing power in the network, so it will always produce new blockchain entries the fastest. However, this is believed to be beyond the capability of any single party, or too expensive to be worth undertaking.
- Bitcoin gets its value from its independence of central authority, its finite limit and the gradual lowering of its supply, and the need to mine it in a difficult process.

- The block reward is halved every four years, until all 21 million bitcoins that will ever exist have been mined. After this point, miners' sole reward will be through the fees gained from approving transactions.
- While any Internet-connected computer can theoretically run bitcoin-mining software, the mining itself has become so specialised, costly and energy-intensive that it is not recommended for home PC users.

Notes

[1] Interestingly, Nakamoto wrote his paper in OpenOffice, an open-source alternative to Microsoft's Office software suite. For more on the open-source movement, you can Google the term—and try its products such as photo editors (GIMP), productivity suites (OpenOffice) or entire operating systems (Linux or Ubuntu) for yourself.

[2] "What is Cryptocurrency: Everything You Need To Know [Ultimate Guide]," BlockGeeks, (no date), at https://blockgeeks.com/guides/what-is-cryptocurrency.

[3] Margaret Rouse and Donna Wolff, "Definition: Peer-to-Peer," *TechTarget SearchNetworking*, at http://searchnetworking.techtarget.com/definition/peer-to-peer.

[4] Alexey Malanov, "Blockchain, Simplified," *Kaspersky Lab Daily*, 8 September 2016, at https://www.kaspersky.com/blog/bitcoin-easy-explanation/12915.

[5] Satoshi Nakamoto, forum post on 7 August 2010, at https://bitcointalk.org/index. php?topic=721.msg8114#msg8114.

[6] Niccolo Machiavelli, *The Prince: A New Translation by Tim Parks* (New York, NY: Penguin Classics, 2009), "Conquered by Alexander the Great, the Kingdom of Darius did not rebel against his successors after his death. Why not?"

[7] Ibid.

[8] Altcoins, of course, are positioned based on this process (among other factors). LiteCoin is said to be the silver to Bitcoin's gold, and achieves this by being released more frequently and easier to mine.

[9] Steven Roose, "Why is mining necessary for the Bitcoin network/system?" *StackExchange*, 28 April 2013, at https://bitcoin.stackexchange.com/ questions/10343/why-is-mining-necessary-for-the-bitcoin-network-system.

CHAPTER 3

A BLOCKCHAINED WORLD

> Bitcoin is first and foremost a currency; this is one particular
> application of a blockchain. However, it is far from the only
> application. To take a past example of a similar situation,
> e-mail is one particular use of the Internet, and for sure
> helped popularise it, but there are many others.[1]
>
> —Dr Gavin Wood, Co-founder of Ethereum

Just like any other product, cryptos are subject to changing needs.
"While bitcoin has captured the attention of currency traders
and investors, the Ethereum ether blockchain was designed with
additional features intended to appeal to the corporate world,"
explains Wayne Duggan at Benzinga.[2]

Ethereum is widely known as Bitcoin's potential successor. It
isn't just a cryptocurrency, but an entire ecosystem of apps built
on a blockchain. It was originally envisioned by Bitcoin developer
Vitalik Butarin, who wanted Bitcoin to have a dedicated scripting
language. Failing to find community support for his idea, he found
corporate partners eager to take the idea in new directions.

Ethereum isn't just Bitcoin 2.0. The two are similar in that
both are decentralised, worldwide blockchain networks, but that's
where the similarity ends. Bitcoin's blockchain is simply a record

of financial transactions, but Ethereum is seen as an ecosystem of applications, in which the blockchain runs their code.

This means that unlike apps on Windows, Google Play or the App Store, Ethereum's applications—which are envisioned to be the next generation after Oracle, WhatsApp and more—are linked by a common blockchain and cross-compatibility from the beginning.

Ethereum itself can be thought of as the open world in *Minecraft*—a bare-bones blockchain on which anything can be built.

In other words, Bitcoin is but one application of a blockchain, while Ethereum is a generalised blockchain that any app developer can use for their own purposes.

Ethereum 101

Ethereum is powered by its own cryptocurrency, known as *ether* (ETH), which is used for transaction fees and buying services on Ethereum's network. Resources are allocated for operations based on their cost in another unit known as *gas*.

As such, Ethereum startups typically raise money in the form of ether—it can be bought and sold on many of the same exchanges as Bitcoin. If we compare bitcoins to notes of cash, ether would be like notes embedded with smart chips.

Ethereum operations are known as *smart contracts*, which are simply immutable, self-operating programmes that watch for the specific conditions that trigger them, then activate certain operations such as sending money or trading a property. "The individuals involved are anonymous, but the contract is in the public ledger," writes Bernardo Nicoletti, author of *The Future of Fintech*. "Regulators can use the blockchain to understand the activity in the market while maintaining the privacy of individual actors' positions."[3]

Another use of Ethereum almost proved to be its undoing. A collection of smart contracts can be organised into a Decentralised Autonomous Organisation (DAO), and in June 2016, one such DAO was hacked, with the (still-unknown) thieves capturing one-sixth of all the ether in the world.

I'll share more about the hack itself in the next chapter; in the meantime, all you need to know is that the community grew divided over what should be done to help those who lost their investments. One camp wanted the entire blockchain 'rolled back' with every transaction and block created since the hack, and all the stolen ether sealed away so it could never be used; the other wanted to preserve the principle of blockchain immutability, and do nothing. As David Siegel describes it:

> The only way to "rewrite history" would be to have at least 51 percent of all nodes agree to such a collusion—something that has never happened in the history of Bitcoin or Ethereum. The goal of a decentralised network is that no one has the power to do that, or the network itself becomes untrustworthy.[4]

In the end, the decision was made to split the Ethereum blockchain in two. The former group in favour of 'rolling back' the chain was endorsed by the developers, and kept the Ethereum name. The latter group argued that Ethereum had actually worked the way it was designed, and the 'burnt' investors should not be asking for special treatment. Siegel admits that the rollback amounted to a bailout:

> In a related way, this is why Lehman Brothers was allowed to fail—because the deal is the deal, and if you bend the rules for a particular player, all other players will want special treatment, too [...]
>
> The analogy to the bank bailouts is remarkable: banks were able to take huge risks hoping for huge returns, and when those trades went south, the taxpayers bailed them out (except for poor Lehman Brothers). This risk asymmetry is generally thought of as a bad way to incentivise market participants.[5]

The latter camp kept the existing (but no longer compatible) setup under the name Ethereum Classic (ETC). Today, these two chains are in competition, and it's too early to tell who will triumph in the long run.

The Rise of the Smart Contract

"In real life, people do much more with their money rather than just money transfer," notes my partner Loi Luu at Kyber Network. "To name a few, we have money exchange, peer-to-peer and traditional lending, peer-to-peer financing, gambling, investing in companies and projects."

Ethereum's smart contract system is that tool. The term actually predates cryptocurrency—it was coined by Bitcoin pioneer and e-gold proposer Nick Szabo in a now-famous 1995 blog post. A modern polymath, Szabo has a body of work that covers ancient history, law and computer programming and many other fields. Although he denies it, he is one of the figures suspected of being Satoshi Nakamoto.

Szabo was the first to spell out the possibility of computers automatically drawing up and executing transactions based on simple, logical tests. He defined a smart contract as "a set of promises, specified in digital form, including protocols within which the parties perform on these promises."[6] This isn't a formal definition—there actually isn't one—but Ethereum co-founder Butarin uses the following: "A smart contract is a computer programme executed in a secure environment that directly controls digital assets."

In the context of blockchain, it can be adapted into: "... a computer programme executed in a *blockchain* that directly controls *cryptocurrencies and tokens*."

In other words, a smart contract encodes an agreement between parties (and all supporting documents) in the form of a computer programme, which will be executed once the agreed conditions are met. This agreement can be of any type—a loan, a transaction, an investment or anything else. Because it's on blockchain permanently, nothing can be deleted or lost. And due to the decentralised, trustless nature of blockchain, and the extreme difficulty of tampering with it, it's an excellent environment in which to carry out the outcome of the agreement.

How does it work? The following explanation is adapted from Loi's notes.

Suppose the following simple situation. Two netizens, Ayden and Shotaro, have some bitcoins and ether respectively. Each wants to exchange their coin for the other, and both agree on the exchange rate. But how can they do the transfer, since they only know each other's online identity—something that can be easily faked? Without blockchain, they must trust each other—but how does Ayden know Shotaro won't run away with his bitcoins after he makes the transfer? Likewise, how does Shotaro know that Ayden won't take his ether and vanish?

Traditionally, an escrow service (that is, a provider setting up a temporary holding arrangement) is the solution. But that just brings up another question—how do we know the escrow provider can be trusted? Many supposedly fair financial agencies have scammed customers or simply disappeared with their money.

A smart contract removes the need for a trusted escrow service, and with it the possibility of getting scammed. Because it exists on a blockchain, no one can compromise it through hacking without great trouble that would render any gain worthless.

And because the various scenarios are programmed into the smart contract, it can hold the paid coins in an escrow-like deposit and keep track of whether each party has paid up. Then, and only then, will it release the exchanged coins to Ayden and Shotaro. At the same time, it can keep copies of any written agreement they make up, so there is no way information can be 'lost' or 'forgotten'.

So if only Ayden or Shotaro pays, and the other doesn't before an agreed time, the contract will simply return the payer their coins.

Just like in Bitcoin, Ethereum has miners that verify and execute the code of the smart contract to update its state. Assuming the majority of miners are honest (and they have strong incentive to be), Ayden and Shotaro have the guarantee that the contract will be honoured—and that unless both pay, the one who paid will always get back their coins.

Smart Contracts and Legal Agreements

"Isn't that the same as a legal contract?" is a question we're often asked. Sometimes it's phrased, "Does that mean smart contracts will replace lawyers?"

The happy (or sad, depending on your point of view) truth is that lawyers aren't going to go hungry anytime soon—the two fill very different roles. Some key differences include:

- *Machine vs human interpretation.* The logic behind a smart contract consists of simple, static and known rules that a machine can interpret definitively, in the same way that a vending machine accepts your coins, delivers your product and returns you the change. However, legal contracts involve varying relationships between parties, and can be interpreted differently depending on the lawyer, the locality and many other factors—including external ones not included in the original contract.
- *All eventualities as written vs arbitration.* Smart contracts have every possible scenario accounted for—there are holdings of money as collateral, and executions that give results based on simple Yes/No logical tests. This means that the assets are transferred if, and only if, the arranged conditions programmed into the contract are met. On the other hand, legal contracts involve enforcement parties (such as the courts) and the process of arbitration in the case of any disagreement.

By removing the need for corruptible parties, smart contracts open the door for many decentralised processes, including:

- *Money sharing.* This is done through a contract powering a multi-signature wallet. Users can decide policies like approved money recipients; how many votes are required to send a payment and to whom; and how much can be spent per day. This removes the need to trust any single member or authority, as well as the ability of any outsider to compromise the entire fund.

  (A similar arrangement exists in the fiat banking system, but it's more inefficient—the bank will need physical signatures from each person before the transaction can be confirmed. With a smart contract, people can do this anytime and anywhere.)

- *Governance and voting.* A perennial problem in many countries is the reliability of the election system. As a result, voting is a time-consuming process that requires thousands of people to line up, show their identities and fill in forms. Even then, many irregularities and lost votes still happen.

  Smart contracts might solve this problem. By encoding voting policies on the same platform, voters can do so by sending transactions to verify their vote. It is more than possible to ensure privacy by not disclosing voters' choices to each other—and the system is protected from tampering by the blockchain's immutability. At the same time, all transactions are open to audit and public verification by any third party far more easily. Voter fraud therefore becomes much more difficult, with no single point of entry where it can happen.

- *Crypto exchange.* A smart contract network can power an entire exchange system, rendering it much less susceptible to hacking or trust to hold customer's funds. This would address the vulnerabilities that have brought several centralised exchanges down—most notably Mt Gox in 2014.

- *Car-sharing.* Thanks to the self-enforcing nature of smart contracts, blockchain and the Internet of Things (that is, the connection of various household devices to the Internet to share information, besides computers) are set to revolutionise the world of car rental and transportation. Imagine short-service contracts allowing you to rent a self-driving car by sending ether to the car's smart contract—it takes you where you want to go, then is automatically released for the next customer.

  And by automatically sending its money to service providers, the car can literally pay for petrol and maintenance by itself, and drive itself there... all without its owners or any person having to lift a finger.

If Bitcoin was the beginning of blockchain and crypto-currency, Ethereum is how it will take off into general use worldwide. The advent of blockchain effectively adds to the power of the Internet in breaking down barriers—there is no technical reason why everyone on earth cannot take part. In the next chapter, we'll take a look at the social and ethical dimensions that Nakamoto unleashed upon the world.

Your New Blocks

- Blockchain technology is what underpins Bitcoin, and is a revolutionary invention in its own right.
- Ethereum is the first, most successful attempt to set up a blockchain for general use—a decentralised open 'world computer' that anyone can access and use.
- Ethereum's blockchain allows its applications to cross-communicate at all times; its operations use a cryptocurrency called ether.
- Smart contracts are what power Ethereum. They are essentially agreements between parties encoded on the blockchain, which automatically make transactions when the conditions are met.
- Ethereum and smart contracts have numerous real-world applications, which startups are just beginning to explore.

Notes

[1] Quoted in "What is Ethereum? A Step-by-Step Beginners Guide," *BlockGeeks*, (no date), at https://blockgeeks.com/guides/what-is-ethereum.

[2] Wayne Duggan, "The History Of Ethereum, In One Infographic," (no date), *Benzinga*, http://m.benzinga.com/article/9740796

[3] Bernardo Nicoletti, *The Future of FinTech: Integrating Finance and Technology in Financial Services* (New York, NY: Springer, 2017), 242.

[4] David Siegel, "Understanding The DAO Hack for Journalists," *Medium*, 19 June 2016, at https://medium.com/@pullnews/understanding-the-dao-hack-for-journalists-2312dd43e993.

[5] Ibid.

[6] For more on Szabo and his pioneering work, see Michael Gord, "Smart Contracts Described by Nick Szabo 20 Years Ago Now Becoming Reality," *Bitcoin Magazine*, 26 April 2016, at https://bitcoinmagazine.com/articles/smart-contracts-described-by-nick-szabo-years-ago-now-becoming-reality-1461693751.

CHAPTER 4

L'ARGENT SANS FRONTIERES

Thirty years ago... we would probably have banked with a national bank, and left ourselves vulnerable to that nation's government seizing our assets, should they at any stage become hostile to us, as they might well. But global and non-national banking saves us from that risk. Medical corps; we tend to ourselves and to our friends. Technical support, we attend to ourselves. It is much easier to do this, in the interconnected age of knowledge, than you might think—some little training, most of it arranged by the soldiers for themselves, augmented by immediate access to all the world's databases, wikis and resources covers most eventualities. As to staff officers, we have none. We monitor one another. It is, again, in our interests to do this. As to an officer corps: we repudiate so archaic, aristocratical a notion as *commanding officer*. We have no need for that sort of thing.

—Adam Roberts, *New Model Army* (2010)[1]

In this chapter, you'll see:

- Why Bitcoin is such a big deal and worth so much
- What it means for authorities, including central banks and governments
- The implications for you, the owner

The medical organisation *Medicins sans Frontieres* (French for 'Doctors Without Borders') is an international medical corps that doctors and nurses can join for overseas emergency medical work, taking healing into war and disaster zones too isolated or difficult for conventional teams to reach. It can be argued that cryptocurrencies, by their non-national nature, does exactly this for money and economic benefit. Bitcoin is, in a real sense, *l'argent sans frontieres*—money without borders.

Once Nakamoto brought Bitcoin online, for the first time an entire payment system existed beyond the ability of any bank, government or authority to police, and there was truly a store of value that people could call their own.

No More Oversight
A millennia-old scene from the Bible captures the nature of money, oversight and government so well, I'm sure its writers must be having a chuckle somewhere as they watch crypto take off.

In it, a cunning group of religious leaders tries to flatter Jesus Christ, then pose Him a trick question to trap Him in His words. Paraphrased, it goes: "We know that you tell the truth and don't sugar-coat it for anyone. Tell us, should we pay our taxes to Caesar, or not?"[2]

In a world where authority was far more centralised than it is now, that was a dangerous question indeed. This isn't the book to go into the details with, but I'll give you the short version. If Jesus agreed that the tax should be paid, He would be endorsing the often authoritarian practices of Rome, which His fellow Jews hated—and if He did not, they could have Him arrested for inciting rebellion.

Many people, Christians and non-Christians, already know His response. "Show me a denarius (that is, a Roman silver coin). Whose image is on it?"

"Caesar's," they answer.

"Then give to Caesar what is Caesar's, and to God what is God's," Jesus snaps. And there the mike drops, for no one has any answer for Him.

Many people have interpreted this story over the centuries, but here's my (crypto-influenced) take. It's a question of *ownership*.

Just as money was minted in Caesar's name, the Roman emperor and his government could indeed levy taxes on ordinary people who earned, used and invested the said money but who only possessed varying amounts and couldn't be said to truly own it. Think about why we call the regular money in your bank account *fiat*—its existence and value came about by government command.

But the religious leaders' role required them to guide people to serve God, each of whom bore the image of the Divinity Himself. (In Judeo-Christian theology, human beings are God's image-bearers, stamped with some part of His nature.)

In other words, the religious leaders had no business demanding an answer to such a question, as it was beyond their jurisdiction. Serve your purpose, Jesus effectively reminds them, and let Caesar serve his.

But the issue of ownership remains, whether we're dealing with silver coins, bank accounts or blockchains. As we've seen, Caesar owns your fiat currency. But who truly owns and holds power over your crypto, if the only image it carries is your unique, anonymous ID—a nonsense chain of letters and numbers? I don't. Nakamoto doesn't. The miners who verify Bitcoin transactions every 10 minutes don't. God might, but to date He hasn't interfered with how you or I might use it.

That decentralised nature and control is by design, and part of why Nakamoto's concept took off so fast and raised so many hackles. In principle, your crypto is yours forever, and thanks to the incredible amount of encryption placed on blockchains, no bank or government can change that. Your transaction may be taxed, as it will be at your exchange, but as a value store it's yours to keep. That's why it's so valuable, and a big part of the reason it's grown so rapidly in price.

Bitcoin at its heart was designed to remove the need for trust in anyone but yourself, but human nature means that someone, somewhere, will be looking for weak points to attack. It's the same creative impulse that leads to greatness, new technologies and the incredible progress we've made... only turned to the wrong ends. As many a philosopher has noted, the better and more capable a being is of doing good, the worse it can do when it does evil.

Nakamoto believed that trust in monetary authorities means they can (and probably will) take terrible risks with your money, and face no penalty for messing up. The remedy for this, he realised, was to enable money to be stored and managed entirely by its users, and its users alone.

As such, bitcoins aren't created or stored by them, but by you—but as the Spider-Man quote goes, with great power comes great responsibility. Because you are their owner, you are also the sole point of responsibility for what happens to them. If you accidentally lose your wallet or your login info, or make a transaction you want to take back, there is literally no power on earth that can help you short of the recipient sending your coins back. Many exchanges do provide some customer protection, but there is nothing legally compelling them to do so.

"A Donation to Everyone"

Nakamoto was against any redress for people who lost access to their bitcoins. Because bitcoins can only be accessed by their owner using the right credentials, many have been lost through their storage devices being stolen, going missing or thrown out by mistake.[3] Again, because the owner is the sole arbiter of their fate, missing bitcoins can never be used—ever.

"Lost coins only make everyone else's coins worth slightly more," he wrote. "Think of it as a donation to everyone."[4]

But the bottom line is that with so much wealth beyond Caesar's ability to collect, tax and control, whatever he says his reasons are, makes him very nervous indeed.

No More Hierarchies

In 2010, British science fiction author Adam Roberts envisioned a future where the bulk of warfare is done by New Model Armies, or NMAs—leaderless mercenary forces that answer to no government, possess no rank structure and have no centralised command units. Instead, they fight for whomever will pay them to do so; battlefield chatter, co-ordination and training are done entirely online through instant messaging and shared article boards (known as *wikis*), with important decisions taken to a vote between equals.

In other words, through the power of the Internet, an NMA takes roles that would traditionally be given to commanders and decentralises them throughout the entire force. And as we've seen, cryptocurrency perfectly fits Roberts' description of "global and non-national banking". While the novel doesn't mention cryptocurrencies, let alone Bitcoin, there's no doubt that Nakamoto's invention had indeed granted individuals the power to access such banking outside of any authority but themselves.

The result? A more flexible fighting force that can disperse in one area, re-form in another and keep traditional armies on their toes—becoming far harder to contain and destroy, fighting to standstills and outright victories, and inflicting great damage despite its smaller size.

Was Roberts far off the mark? Probably not. Real life soon caught up when the terrorist group known as the Islamic State took over large portions of Iraq and Syria, and set up terror cells all over the world, showing how effective even a crudely decentralised army can be.

If I could sum up the march of technology in one word, it would be *empowerment*. Every revolutionary advance, however mundane it might seem today, has had the effect of giving the many the ability to do things traditionally reserved only for the few. Technology, for better or worse, upends existing power structures and thus enacts sweeping changes to society that were unimaginable before.

History is full of examples:

- Telephones—replacing expensive telegrams and allowing instantaneous communication.

- Cars—making rapid, convenient transportation available to anyone, without the need for expensive, high-maintenance horses and carriages.
- The printing press—creating books quickly and cheaply, making education available to the masses and breaking authorities' stranglehold on knowledge.
- The crossbow and later, the gun—opening up fights (and possible victory) to ordinary people with far less strength and training than professional soldiers and knights.

It is precisely this box that Bitcoin ticks.

Shortly after Nakamoto's proposal, it was suggested that cryptography and politics were completely independent, and he should not hope to change the world through it. "You will not find a solution to political problems in cryptography," a user wrote to him.

"Yes," he answered. "But we can win a major battle in the arms race and gain a new territory of freedom for several years. Governments are good at cutting off the heads of a centrally controlled networks [sic] like Napster, but pure P2P networks like Gnutella and Tor seem to be holding their own.[5]

Bitcoin isn't just a way of storing and transacting dollars and cents. Anyone with an Internet connection in a third-world nation can access Bitcoin exchanges and *immediately* take part in a worldwide marketplace—without passing through authorities like governments and banks, and storing his wealth online in the form of cryptocurrency. One result is that it's become easier than ever to assist small businesses in the developing world, which often are unable to grow due to being cut off from stable, reliable financial services.

And by increasing participation in the world economy, Bitcoin has the potential to grow commerce and create economic booms where fiat money could not, for any number of reasons. With cryptocurrency, you aren't reliant on government fiat to keep your money wherever you choose. Any democratic government that tried to ban or shut Bitcoin down would immediately (and deservedly) face retribution from its own citizens at the ballot box, making the social cost of doing so far too high.

They are realising that, like it or not, their people have the option of storing their wealth in a form that cannot be struck down by their regulators. As Roberts' narrator notes on the similarity of NMAs to city-states in themselves:

> This is one of the mistakes made by those generals who have gone to war against New Model Armies. They think they are fighting a corps of men and women. They are not. They are fighting a *polis*. That is why they lose.[6]

No More Coercion

Cryptocurrency's main strength is that no one party controls how they function. Their creators simply lay down a set of rules, and leave the system to be run by its users and miners. How does Bitcoin stay on track, despite having no one to call the shots?

By leaving compliance with its rules to the discretion of individual users, *and* making all its architecture open-source—so that anyone who is unhappy is free to start their own competing coin. In other words, if you want to keep enjoying what Bitcoin has to offer, it's in your best interests to follow the rules and run the same software as everyone else. Otherwise, the opportunity is there for you make your own rules through your own 'copy' of the crypto.

This is why entrepreneurial coach Taylor Pearson argues that while Bitcoin may be a new technology, its democratising effect means we should be thinking in terms of the march towards greater individual freedom. As he observes on Coindesk:

> Cryptocurrency governance systems may be at a stage analogous to the Articles of Confederation era, when the country was trying a new system of governance that seemed promising, but still had major kinks to be worked out [...]
>
> In the same way the Internet enabled permissionless innovation by allowing anyone to create a website without asking permission, forking allows anyone to create their own network without asking permission. It's A/B testing on steroids.[7]

Pearson compares the crypto ecosystem to employees at a company with three other job offers on the table. Because cryptos live or die on mining and community participation, people always have the choice of staying and improving existing systems, or walking away and taking key assets—and replicate the whole thing on their own terms should they so choose. As a result, they can be far more vocal about their objections, and developers will have little choice but to listen to them.

On the other hand, walking away and setting up your own coin comes with its own set of risks. If no one buys into this vision, the new coin is more likely to lose value and die a natural death—as has been the fate of thousand of Bitcoin clones. This, in effect, is how a decentralised network manages to enforce its own rules, and punish failure to follow them.

No More Lack of Financial Services

We've seen that because the root technology behind cryptocurrency is open-source, anyone is free to create their own. That's exactly how many startups are choosing to fundraise—rather than issue stocks or seek out venture capitalists, they set up a custom blockchain and issue their own cryptocurrency (or '*token*') in what is known as an Initial Coin Offering (ICO). However, note that while many are genuine, there are also many scams; the usual rules of due diligence apply.

Caesar is working to put whatever control over the network he can, as this system is unfortunately open to abuse. Remember that while he cannot tamper with cryptos themselves, he can regulate how they are bought and sold to a large extent.

The crypto market suffered a shock in late September 2017, when the Chinese government issued a blanket ban on ICO investment by exchanges inside the country. Overnight, crypto prices, Bitcoin and all, crashed as investors sold off what seemed to be a losing asset.[8] (As of this writing, other governments have pledged to do so, or actually banned ICOs altogether.)

"On Monday morning, China said cryptocurrencies had 'seriously disrupted the economic and financial order' and outlawed Initial Coin Offerings (ICOs)—also known as token sales—the means by which funds are raised for a new cryptocurrency venture," writes Joseph Hincks at *Time*.

Bitcoin lost over 11% in the 24 hours before time of writing, Ethereum and Litecoin had plunged almost 20%, and Ripple nosedived 14%. Some, like EOS and Qtum, had lost almost 40%. Among the larger coins, only Tether—the 19th largest cryptocurrency by market cap— was holding out with a 3.2% gain.[9]

Combined with an American warning against the legality of some ICOs (a polite way of saying, "Beware of scams"), and the provocative behaviour of North Korea, investors were driven to put their money in more 'reliable' financial products, such as gold. It took a week for finance officials to 'clarify' that the ban would be temporary, until they worked out what controls and regulations to place on crypto trading.

It may be a single incident, but crypto's very novelty means that governments and regulators will always be trying to play catch-up. This hasn't been the first case of a government strong-arming the crypto trade, and it won't be the last. This is one sense in which crypto's lack of oversight is both a strength and a weakness— because of this, it is uniquely valuable to people, but also uniquely vulnerable to their behaviour.

The flow of money across borders is stemmed by restrictions on how much you can carry in cash. Fill out any customs card, and you'll notice that any amount above, say, $10,000 or its equivalent needs to be declared. "China, for example, is the world's second-largest economy, yet individuals may not withdraw more than $50,000 per annum from the country," says Frisby.[10]

Nowhere is Bitcoin more in demand than countries facing economic trouble. In 2013, a banking crisis in Cyprus saw its price shoot up from $15 to $200, and even more once Chinese investors got interested.[11] By making international payment much faster and easier, Bitcoin has changed the game; it's giving the bigger, less efficient bureaucracies that run central banks and impose capital controls a run for their money.

Others have taken an approach summed up as: "If you can't beat them, join them." Responses include taking a hands-off approach to cryptocurrencies, setting up exchanges or even creating their own coins to let people invest in their countries. There are of course exceptions, such as South Korea, which might seek to ban crypto trading on its domestic exchanges.[12] (However, such governments do face pushback at the ballot box, if enough people feel forced or strong-armed into giving up their crypto.)

In comparison, financial institutions continue to be slow in adopting the growth of crypto and blockchain. A majority of startups report challenges in opening accounts and transacting in fiat currencies with investors, likely arising from philosophical clashes as banks are centred around knowing your customer, while crypto keeps things trust-free and pseudonymous. A case in point: in early 2016, my friend and I sent instruction to invest US$50,000 into Melonport through a foreign bank only to have them come back with an alibi five days later that the transaction failed to go through.

The reason? Compliance failed to recognise the name Bitcoin Suisse, the very currency needed to convert our investment into. As a result, we lost the opportunity to invest, and our very initial outlay would have been worth US$1 million in return by now!

No More Gatekeepers

Seen the BBC TV series *Dragon's Den,* or its US version *Shark Tank?* If not, here's the lowdown: Entrepreneurs make their pitches for new business ventures in front of rich investors called 'dragons' or 'sharks', who offer their partnership in exchange for shares of the business if they see potential. This is basically televising the traditional model of startup funding known as venture capital.

However, ICOs mean that startups can invite potential customers to participate as direct investors in the business. It is hoped that as business takes off, their coins will grow more valuable and desirous to people, in the same way shares of Apple or Facebook are today.

Before dismissing ICOs, consider the fact that by early 2017, they had set up a market worth over $1 billion. However, as of this writing, they are not considered financial instruments, investments or any kind of regulated commodity. But part of the reason they've been so successful is because they're so easy to set up; the best startups have literally raised hundreds of millions of dollars in minutes.

I'm listing this effect last because of the massive uncertainty attached to them—and I've run them myself! As economist John Koetsier explains on *Inc*:

Entrepreneurs and startups that want to launch an ICO typically create a company, build their startup to an early stage, announce their plan to launch a token sale, and publish a white paper about what they intend to create, how they intend to do it, and how much money they need to make it happen. [...] It helps—just like in crowdfunding on Kickstarter or Indiegogo—if early investors get a good deal.[13]

Of course, while many ICOs are legitimate, because they're so easy to set up, scams abound and the entire system is expected to become a bubble. These aren't baseless accusations, as startups are effectively creating an entirely new store of value with no backing from any tangible resource. And because Bitcoin and other, more established cryptocurrencies are so volatile, an ICO's funding can rise and fall practically overnight. Koetsier points out that:

> For example, Tezos raised $220 million in four days, but when Bitcoin went down in value, it dropped to $142 million, even as the company continued to raise. As Bitcoin recovered, the amount went back up... but the risk remains.
>
> And even "secure" and "mature" cryptocurrencies like Bitcoin and Ethereum could be dragged down in the wake of a massive loss of confidence in ICOs in general. Just this past week, the entire cryptocurrency market cap dropped $13 billion in a single day, thanks largely to disputes within the Bitcoin community over how to scale the technology for the future.[14]

What can be made of ICOs? "At the moment, it is very difficult to justify the market value of the entire ICO market and its projects. Their value is completely speculative and can't be evaluated with real market data because no viable products or software have been deployed yet," notes Joseph Young of CoinTelegraph. And in order to support the expected millions of users, sweeping changes will have to be made to the Ethereum network.[15]

In other words: It's too early to tell.

Much remains unknown, so treat ICO trading like you would the stock of a risky startup. Maybe it will succeed; maybe it won't. Don't ignore ICOs completely, but don't give in to greed, or invest so much you lose sleep over what might happen.

It remains to be seen how governments and monetary authorities make their peace with crypto, but many are seeking not to control it themselves, but protect their citizens from the risks. They've acknowledged it's here to stay—and empower people without conventional access to world markets in the same way that gold did a generation ago.

Your New Blocks

- Cryptocurrencies are about breaking down barriers—be they national borders, hindrances to human co-operation and government control.
- Unlike fiat money, your cryptocurrency is your own to use. No central authority controls how you can or cannot use it.
- By allowing millions of people without access to world markets a store of value, especially in the developing world, Bitcoin and its fellow cryptos are set to empower people in new ways we are only beginning to find out.

- Bitcoin doesn't need to be policed by a central authority, its developers or anyone else. Instead, compliance is guaranteed by mutual self-interest; anyone in the network must be running a recognised version of the Bitcoin software to participate. Otherwise, they are free to modify Bitcoin's architecture, and start their own competing cryptocurrency.

- Governments are unable to shut down cryptocurrencies at a single point, and are instead working to regulate citizens' access and prevent scams.

- ICOs are mechanisms for startup companies to raise funds through selling custom cryptocurrencies. Governments are working to protect citizens through various regulatory means, but it is best to exercise your own due diligence.

Notes

[1] Adam Roberts, *New Model Army* (London, UK: Gollancz, 2010).

[2] The story is found in the Gospel of Matthew, Chapter 22.

[3] For a warning of what can go wrong, see: Mark Frauenfelder, "I Forgot my PIN: An Epic Tale of Losing $30,000 in Bitcoin," *Wired*, 29 October 2017, at https://www.wired.com/story/i-forgot-my-pin-an-epic-tale-of-losing-dollar30000-in-bitcoin.

[4] Satoshi Nakamoto, "Dying bitcoins," 21 June 2010, at https://bitcointalk.org/index. php?topic=198.msg1647#msg1647

[5] Satoshi Nakamoto, "Re: Bitcoin P2P e-cash paper," Cryptography Mailing List, 7 November 2008, at bit.ly/1truasJ.

[6] Roberts, *New Model Army*.

[7] Taylor Pearson, "You Want Democracy? Try a Hard Fork," *Coindesk*, 15 November 2017, at https://www.coindesk.com/you-want-real-democracy-try-a-hard-fork.

[8] Hannah Boland, "Bitcoin price falls further amid China crackdown," *The Telegraph*, 14 September 2017, at http://www.telegraph.co.uk/technology/2017/09/14/bitcoin-price-falls-amid-china-crackdown.

[9] Joseph Hincks, "Virtually Every Cryptocurrency in the World Is Tanking Right Now," *Time*, 5 September 2017, at http://time.com/4926712/cryptocurrency-crash-bitcoin-ethereum-ether-investing-ripple.

[10] Frisby, *Bitcoin, The Future of Money?*

[11] Ibid.

[12] Dahee Kim and Cynthia Kim, "South Korea plans to ban cryptocurrency trading, rattles market," *Channel NewsAsia*, 11 January 2018, at https://www.channelnewsasia.com/news/ south-korea-plans-to-ban-cryptocurrency-trading--rattles-market-9851302.

[13] John Koetsier, "ICO Bubble? Startups Are Raising Hundreds of Millions of Dollars Via Initial Coin Offerings," Inc, 14 July 2017, at https://www.inc.com/john-koetsier/ico-bubble-startups-are-raising-hundreds-of-millio.html.

[14] Ibid.

[15] Joseph Young, "ICO Market Crosses $1 Billion Mark, Is Bubble Imminent?" *CoinTelegraph*, 9 July 2017, at https://cointelegraph.com/news/ico-market-crosses-1-billion-mark-is-bubble-imminent.

CHAPTER 5

MONEY TALKS :
NAVIGATING THE CRAZY WORLD OF ALTCOINS

> There is only one boss. The customer. And he can fire
> everybody in the company from the chairman on down,
> simply by spending his money somewhere else.
>
> —Sam Walton, Founder of Wal-Mart

Just as the personal computer began at IBM but didn't stay there,
Bitcoin isn't the be all and end all of cryptocurrency. In fact,
competition was built into the market from the very beginning. In the
same way that computers have expanded to fill every possible niche
and serve a range of different customers, cryptos are no different—
as financial products, they are affected by the same forces of supply
and demand as anything else. Seeing Bitcoin's dramatic rise in value,
many companies have developed their own cryptocurrencies. It is
hoped that these will do Bitcoin's job, or better.

Why Altcoins?
It bears remembering that just because you can use bitcoin for your
day-to-day payments, it doesn't mean you should. One of the side
effects of the mining system is that it is the same money-hungry
miners whose computers release new bitcoins that determine

if your transaction goes through. We've seen that because they must divert a portion of their CPU power to do this, they are incentivised in the form of a block reward, and all transaction fees for those transactions they include within that block. Think of this as the service charge at a restaurant.

Imagine that you're going to a hugely popular restaurant, the kind where you need to book seats months in advance. Unfortunately, word has got out how amazing the food is, and so the place is over-booked and a line snakes out the door.

Now the advantage this restaurant has is its decentralised management. Its owners might make decisions, but they cannot act on them without the cooks and waiters buying in. It becomes so successful, with happy staff members earning so much and customers served so well that its stock price rises, and more and more people show up.

Like any network, our restaurant has a limited capacity. The place can only handle 50 orders an hour, but to clear the backlog, it'll have to handle 100.

That's how Bitcoin ran into a scalability problem in June 2016. Just like in our restaurant (Bitcoin's network itself), the chefs and wait staff (miners) are facing more orders (transactions) than they can fill. Each order is the same size (Bitcoin's 1 MB, a limit set by Nakamoto to encourage easier uptake).

Worse, they can't simply have customers (you) eating out in the street—they must seat you at one of the very few tables (blocks) that become available from time to time, as previous customers finish their food and leave.

Now some of the smarter restaurant staff realise that they have to prioritise orders somehow, and the best way to do that is to demand a higher tip. "Attention all guests," they announce. "Due to unforeseen demand, we are placing a bidding system in place. Those who are willing to pay more on their service charge will be seated and served first."

Note that because of the restaurant's decentralised structure, they don't need permission or even announcement to do this—they simply need to act that way for everyone to notice.

Now because customers want their food quickly, they have an incentive to pay more for it to be served promptly.

That was what ended up happening to many Bitcoin users, with transaction fees rising as high as $7. So many transactions occurred that miners began prioritising users who had specified higher transfer fees, and those who couldn't pay faced much longer wait times—effectively limiting the convenience of Bitcoin to the highest bidders. Imagine a restaurant where most of your bill is for the right to be served first... if at all!

Unfair? Discriminatory? Perhaps. But like it or not, bitcoin transactions had to get through, and blocks had to keep being mined at a constant (or near constant) rate for the entire system to work.

Bitcoin's developers (i.e. our restaurant owners, no doubt suffering from poor Yelp reviews or loss of their Michelin stars) were in a bind.

At first, they try to solve the problem by increasing the number of meals per table that can be served by only checking diners' identities after their meal. (This is analogous to a proposal by Bitcoin Core to separate the identity check on each block, which was taking up most of its disk space. It became known as Segregated Witness, or SegWit for short; it will have been implemented by the time you read this.)

Eventually, a longer-term solution is raised. Transaction rates, it is argued, can be sped up by raising the amount of data per block—i.e. seating more diners at a shared table. However, this move would reduce the service charge, removing the incentive for cooks and wait staff to do their best. (Remember, they too are in it to be paid.) In fact, there's the danger that limiting the service charge will make them leave and find work elsewhere; for the purposes of our analogy, switching to mining a more flexible crypto.

Also, this cannot be done without violating the market positioning of the restaurant—and so it's decided that the load will be best placed on an entirely new restaurant, one positioned specially to handle it.

That, in a nutshell, is why Bitcoin Cash (abbreviated BCH in exchanges) was born. Bitcoin users were alerted to the new, completely independent currency (which would branch off from Bitcoin's chain in a '*hard fork*'). A second hard fork came in November 2017 to create a Bitcoin alternative that could be home-mined instead of relying on mining farms. This one is known as Bitcoin Gold (BCG).

Now just as you can go to different restaurants, there's nothing stopping you from having amounts of Bitcoin, Bitcoin Cash and Bitcoin Gold, or any combination of the three. If Bitcoin is an exclusive, reservation-only three-starred restaurant, Bitcoin Cash is a long-tabled family diner where guests are encouraged to come in large groups. On the other hand, Bitcoin Gold resembles a self-serviced buffet where you can collect and cook meals for yourself and others.

Altcoins Everywhere

Notice the difference in views not only over administration, but such fundamental issues like blockchain immutability, lack of central oversight and many more. Blockchain was becoming not only a new Internet-based tool, but a centre of belief with competing visions and ethical ideals. Even today, Bitcoin is split between users who see it as a store of value to be kept and held, and others who want it to be easily carried around and spent as a replacement of fiat money. Again, it's too early to tell which side will win out.

But like new players moving into a crowded market, altcoins spy out a good niche they can occupy. As Frisby writes:

> In a few years, just as we have different apps on our phones, so will we have different "wallets" with different currencies: one we might use for tipping (dogecoin), another for transactions we want kept private (monero, zcash), another for fast transactions and so on.[1]

We've already met Ethereum, which looks like it could dethrone Bitcoin in the near future. Here are some other cryptos worth watching:

- *Litecoin* (LTC) is marketed as the 'silver to Bitcoin's gold,' in the words of its creator, ex-Googler Charlie Lee.[2] "Think of litecoin as the change in your pocket, and bitcoin as your large assets and savings," writes Andrew Torba of Coindesk.[3] As of this writing, one litecoin's value is in the low three-digit range.

Designed to be easier to mine and transact, Litecoin features a much shorter block generation time (2.5 minutes, compared to Bitcoin's 10), and will be capped at 84 million coins—exactly four times Bitcoin's limit of 21 million. It is famous for solving the speed limitation of Bitcoin, even before Bitcoin itself did. It is also the first major coin to support the SegWit and Lightning Network protocols, and like Bitcoin, it is being accepted by more and more merchants around the world.

- *Dash* (DASH; formerly known as DarkCoin and XCoin) aims to both protect users' anonymity, and allow them to transact instantly and nearly untraceably. By removing the delay that comes from waiting for Bitcoin's miners to approve user transactions, Dash has built up a growing and passionate group of users.

- *Zcash* (ZEC) is billed as a secure alternative to Bitcoin, and while transaction amounts remain on a blockchain, users have the option to encrypt those and 'shield' them using additional cryptography.

  "These constructions ensure validity of transactions as well as secure ledger of balances without giving out any other information (such as parties or amount involved). Thus Zcash offers an added feature over bitcoin, while ensuring that nobody is cheating or stealing," writes Prableen Bajpai at *Investopedia*.[4]

  In other words, the only publicly accessible part of Zcash (its blockchain) will only show that a transaction took place, not the identities and histories of the people involved, or the amount.

- *Ripple* (XRP) was designed to be a global network of payment transfers, providing greater transparency with lower associated costs. It is unique in that it does not get mined, saving computer power; rather, some is permanently lost with every transaction. "Ripple is unique in that it allows for transacting with any unit of value, from fiat currency to frequent flier miles," writes Anthony Coggine at CoinTelegraph.com.[5]

- *Monero* (XMR) is set up to provide anonymity, although in a different way from Dash; even its blockchain does not publicly show every transaction that takes place. Unfortunately, this has led to great popularity on the Dark Web, and among criminals.

No book can keep up-to-date with the thousands of cryptocurrencies that come and go. But every new entrant into the market succeeds or fails based on the same principles of product, positioning and performance. In other words, the same competitive process that has driven business since one vegetable farmer realised he had an advantage that his rivals did not, and vice versa.

Will Bitcoin Stay the Top Dog?
"There can only ever be 21 million Bitcoins. Bitcoin is designed to be a form of electronic money and nothing else," writes Danny Bradbury at financial site The Balance. "These are all conscious

choices that were made when the bitcoin protocol was originally designed, but there's nothing that says those rules can't change."[6]

There are, at present, three schools of thought surrounding altcoins:

- Bitcoin is king—there is no reason to ever buy altcoins.

- Ethereum or some other altcoin will take the top spot from Bitcoin one day.

- A bubble will cause the crypto market to burst, toppling all but a few players—and a more even power struggle will result.

The bottom line is that Bitcoin is not going down without a fight. "Mostly, people get into altcoins as a way to hedge against Bitcoin," writes Bitcoin developer Jimmy Song on Medium. Some reasons he cites for buying them are in case Bitcoin catastrophically fails; an altcoin does something they want better than Bitcoin; or it might conceivably overtake Bitcoin in the future.

However, Song notes that because Bitcoin is still evolving, a useful feature in other altcoins can easily be incorporated into a Bitcoin-based system if the community finds it to be so. In that case:

It's unlikely that Bitcoin would add [a new coin's] features in directly (though with sidechains, I suppose you can't even rule that out). But there is a strong possibility that some entrepreneur would create a similar service based on

Bitcoin. [...] The barrier of entry would be less, the user base more, so in the end, the new Bitcoin service would have built in network effect advantages that [the coin] wouldn't have.[7]

While altcoins have their place, for them to try to take on Bitcoin is an entirely different challenge altogether... and given Bitcoin's in-built advantages, one they are unlikely to win.

That said, if you find an altcoin works better for you—such as Dash's anonymity, or Ethereum's versatility and use in the future— by all means experiment with them. You can buy Bitcoin and most altcoins through the process I describe in Appendix 1.

Fun With Funding

If you're thinking of participating in an ICO, be on the lookout for scams; only trust those companies with solid business plans and a strong community presence with your hard-earned money.

Many scammers simply impersonate better-known developers or run off with money without ever creating a usable product. Because the blockchain space is so new, it's not unusual for even a genuinely great company not to have any product to show yet. Worse, many scammers co-opt the identities of genuine founders— Loi Luu of Kyber Network has had his biography copied word-for-word and put up under a scammer's name!

It can be hard to tell them apart early on. How do you recognise a bona fide, world-changing ICO with the best potential to make you rich? Here are some signs to look out for:

They get involved in the community by attending and organising meetups. There's probably a cryptocurrency meetup in or near your

Realtime Crowdsale Information

Total ETH Raised	257034.735218840269081188
Total USD Raised (Modifier Applied)	$3,934,836.62
Actual USD Raised	$3,026,798.94
Current Modifier	1.3
Next Round	Thu, 07 Apr 2016 00:00:00 GMT

Join The Crowdsale

Realtime Crowdsale Information

Total ETH Raised	281838.122183445298480188
Total USD Raised (Modifier Applied)	$4,314,240.96
Actual USD Raised	$3,318,648.61
Current Modifier	1.3
Next Round	Thu, 07 Apr 2016 00:00:00 GMT

Join The Crowdsale

Realtime Crowdsale Information

Total ETH Raised	465134.95647440119024894
Total USD Raised (Modifier Applied)	$7,149,996.50
Actual USD Raised	$5,499,999.97
Current Modifier	1.3
Next Round	Thu, 07 Apr 2016 00:00:00 GMT

Join The Crowdsale

Realtime Crowdsale Information

Total ETH Raised	465134.95988259769024894
Total USD Raised (Modifier Applied)	$7,149,996.53
Actual USD Raised	$5,500,000.00
Current Modifier	1.3
Next Round	Thu, 07 Apr 2016 00:00:00 GMT

Join The Crowdsale

Screenshot captures of the DigixDAO Crowdsale.

area; often, the key organisers will be blockchain startup leaders making themselves available. "We picked specific markets to enter, then tried to establish a physical connection by going to meetups to introduce Kyber Network and share what it is," says Tsun Ngai of Kyber. "We'd record a video or live stream, then publish it on YouTube. We also arranged interview sessions with reputable YouTube channels."

They do extensive community outreach even before asking for a single dollar. "Before we did our ICO, we went into marketing it up," says Shaun Djie, COO at Digix, which successfully raised 465,134 ether, or approximately US$5,500,000 then. "We tapped into our old friends in the space, people who were running podcasts and online media. We contacted them to get the word out, and explain to people what we were doing."

Even then, they realise it may not be enough and actively seek community feedback. "In February 2016, a month before our actual sale, we released our white paper on Reddit and Slack. We received a lot of criticism on how we are asking too much from the community, so we had to go back to the drawing board and revise it within 24 hours."

They have clear policies and structure. "We might mirror democracy by saying, 'If you have a certain number of tokens, or if you have been participating actively in making the right decisions for this new corporate governance, then you get more weight; you get more say in the future of our company,'" says Digix CEO Chng Kai Cheng.

They communicate clearly and quickly, with well-written instructions for everyone. "We had to put instructions up on how to participate, and publish guides in English, Arabic and Chinese—and we were still having to clear customer tickets by the second," Shaun says. "We set out to reach our goal in 30 days... only to do it after just 14 hours!"

They make their records known to the public, and do not overpromise. "This product is still in a work in progress, so we made a promise to all our token holders not to spend their money until the whole governance structure was ready," Shaun says. "Anyone with an Internet connection can actually just go online and see that this money has not been touched since the raise happened. It's a sign of trust and transparency, and that we keep our promises."

They proactively educate everyone. "We shared on the security aspect of things," says Tsun Ngai. "Scams were coming out and hackers were sending spoof messages over Slack, with fake Ether addresses to send tokens to. Then they'd claim that the sale had been pushed forward and promise bonuses to those who bought now. What we countered with was never to use email, limit our communication channels and train people to be sceptical of any URL domain they saw—basically questioning the source and doing something about fraud if they spotted it."

Ironically, developing in a trustless environment means trust between investor and developer must be earned and justified every step of the way. "We're moving in very uncharted territory, like crashing through a jungle," Shaun says. "We don't know what the end point is, we don't know what kind of wildlife, monsters or vegetation there will be. That's what it's like developing on Ethereum."

Remember that barring a miracle, you'll probably need to wait a long time before your investment gets results one way or another. "Projects that raised money ahead of us have had to delay their launches, so that something scheduled for 2016 might be pushed back to 2017 or even 2018. That's actually quite normal in this space," he warns. "A lot of things aren't within our control; we can't just ask Ethereum, 'Hey, can you fix this blockchain?' We can't point fingers, only wait for them to get it corrected."

The short version is that the community doesn't just need your money; it needs your participation. None of this replaces going to meetups and doing your homework before contributing, so find one near you and get started today.

Your New Blocks

- Altcoins are simply alternative cryptocurrencies to Bitcoin. Generally, each takes one or more of Bitcoin's advantages, and tries to do it better.
- As of this writing, the top cryptos (out of thousands in existence) include Litecoin (designed to be easier to mine and spend in smaller amounts), Ether (designed to power Ethereum-based apps), Ripple (facilitating international value transfers), Zcash and Monero (strengthening privacy and anonymity).
- Some are born out of ethical and technical limitations in parent coins, such as Bitcoin.
- Cash and Ethereum Classic.
- Bitcoin is unlikely to lose its top spot, and retains a number of key advantages including a large user base, support for entrepreneurs building bitcoin-based systems, and many more.

- Bottom line: A crypto portfolio is a strong value store, although the exact makeup depends on your own strategy and risk appetite.
- ICOs can be a great way to invest in a startup without breaking the bank, but do your homework and only fund reputable companies.

Notes

[1] Dominic Frisby, "Don't let the bankers fool you: bitcoin is here to stay," *The Guardian*, 15 September 2017, at https://www.theguardian.com/commentisfree/2017/sep/15/jp-morgan-ceo-wrong-bitcoin-jamie-dimon.

[2] Robert McMillan, "Ex-Googler Gives the World a Better Bitcoin," *Wired Business*, 30 August 2013, at https://www.wired.com/2013/08/litecoin.

[3] Andrew Torba, "Is Litecoin the Silver to Bitcoin's Gold?" *Coindesk*, 27 November 2013, at https://www.coindesk.com/litecoin-silver-bitcoins-gold.

[4] Prableen Bajpai, "What Is Zcash?" *Investopedia*, 10 November 2016, at https://www.investopedia.com/news/what-zcash.

[5] Anthony Coggine, "Top 10 Altcoins: All You Wanted to Know About Bitcoin's Contenders," *CoinTelegraph*, 28 April 2017, at https://cointelegraph.com/news/top-10-altcoins-all-you-wanted-to-know-about-bitcoins-contenders.

[6] Danny Bradbury, "Altcoins: A Basic Guide," *The Balance*, 14 October 2016, at https://www.thebalance.com/altcoins-a-basic-guide-391206.

[7] Jimmy Song, "Why Bitcoin is Different than other Cryptocurrencies," 16 May 2017, Medium, at https://medium.com/@jimmysong/why-bitcoin-is-different-than-other-cryptocurrencies-e16b17d48b94.

CHAPTER 6

THE OTHER HALF OF THE TRUTH

> So, Lone Starr, now you see that evil will always triumph,
> because good is dumb!
>
> —Dark Helmet, *Spaceballs* (1987)

In its short existence, many myths and half-truths have grown up around Bitcoin and its younger cousins. Note that not all of them come from detractors—not everyone who promotes a crypto understands the concept all that well anyway. For them, crypto is as much an object of ideology and ethics as it is of currency, a trait arguably shared by creator Satoshi Nakamoto himself. As we've seen, Bitcoin's entire creation was inspired by one man's loss of faith in the world financial system, and his creation of what he believed to be a better way.

In this chapter, I'll be sharing some misconceptions pushed by cryptocurrency opponents, a group that has included JPMorgan Chase's Jamie Dimon (whom we met in the Introduction) and legendary investor Warren Buffett. "Stay away from it," the Berkshire Hathaway chief warned in 2014. "It's a mirage, basically."[1] Some of the *FUD* around crypto does have a grain of truth in it, but it's best to learn the whole story first.

In the next chapter, I'll cover half-truths thrown out by crypto's supporters—those people who paint a rosy picture of a currency completely free from government intervention, and believe that blockchains herald the end of state power. (Word from the inside: Blockchain technology, as applied to money, limits state power and forces it to act in a different way... but Caesar isn't going to lose his influence anytime soon.)

As we'll see, the only thing that harms potential investors more than paranoia over what crypto isn't is a misconception of what crypto is, and what it can do.

Claim One: "It doesn't exist! How can it have any value?"
Crypto has value in the sense that people want it and are willing to pay for it. Because demand for say, bitcoins outstrips their supply, its price has grown to thousands of dollars. The coins themselves have no physical presence, but because there is only a limited supply of them, people want to keep them as a value store. Many other factors work together to drive the price of a crypto up or down, such as how difficult it is to mine, its utility in buying things and public perception, especially in the wake of key events like the Mt Gox hack or China's temporary ban.

Think of it this way—the notes in your wallet have no inherent value, as they're just pieces of paper. We as a society simply attach value to them because we worked to earn them (like Bitcoin miners' computers); we can buy things with them (like with most value stores, like bank accounts and credit cards) and the government assures us they have the value printed on the front (a process replicated by cryptocurrencies' mining rules).

In other words, for every mechanism that gives precious metals and fiat currency their value, cryptocurrencies replicate it in some way. In fact, if you read the financial pages, these are *exactly* the same factors that make or break the values of more convention-al products, such as stocks and bonds. Nobody argues that those don't have value!

Is Fiat Stable? Yes. Reliable? Probably Not.

It can be argued that fiat currency actually has *less* reliability, as it's highly dependent on the success of the government producing it. Many older Singaporeans will remember the 'banana money' printed by the occupying Japanese, which became practically worthless after their defeat at the Allies' hands. Similarly, many times of political upheaval in history have been accompanied by currency becoming useless overnight, precipitating lootings, robberies and riots.

Michael Hulleman of *Hobo with a Laptop* writes:

And yet Bitcoin has intrinsic value. Much like a startup initial public offering (IPO), for instance —even if that startup isn't profitable, people assign a value to a stock, sight unseen, based on a white paper or an idea and the capability of the people behind it. And that's all fine and well among critics.

Bitcoin has value that is based on one of the strongest human conditions—faith.[2]

Claim Two: "It's way too easy to hack. I'm not putting any money where someone online can just steal it."

Everybody asks about hackers stealing crypto, so I'll address the elephant in the room here. It looks like a big one, and indeed, exchanges have closed and entire crypto operations have had to change the way they work in response to robbery.

That said, does it make crypto a suicide pact? We all know that you shouldn't invest money you aren't prepared to lose, but hold your judgement till we've examined how that happened.

Why does it matter? Because it lets us pinpoint what's happening. After all, if a bank is robbed it makes a lot of difference whether the robbers shot their way into the vault *Grand Theft Auto*-style, or phished customers' and employees' login information. In the former, it's a matter of physical security. In the latter, we must consider the behaviour of not the criminals, but the people they target. For now, let me point out that there's a difference between the bank being robbed and the cash being tampered with.

You've probably seen Westerns where the villains slip on masks, arm themselves and burst into the service area of the town bank. They'll probably cry, "Reach for the sky!" or "This is a stick-up!" Maybe they'll shoot someone too, just to show they're serious.

If they're successful, they make off with as much of the gold in the vault as they can carry. In an age without telephones or the Internet, they could flee to the next state over and be completely anonymous. By the time the furore and manhunts died down, they were able to regroup and strike again.[3]

I'm not going to sugar-coat it. In a major way, until security greatly improves, crypto does represent a return to the Old West. Sadly, Nakamoto couldn't completely remove trust and human failings from a system intended to be used by human beings. Because user IDs are pseudonymous and blockchains are practically immutable, there exists no way to directly identify users within the network, and no way to reverse a transaction once it has been made.

That means that if hackers gain access to your exchange login information, there is literally no power on Earth that can stop them from cleaning it out. Worse, the very nature of many cryptos (Bitcoin included) effectively solves the anonymity problem for them.

There Will Be Casualties

By 2011, exchanges trading Bitcoin and other cryptocurrencies had been set up around the world. One of the largest was Mt Gox, set up by a passionate coder and *Magic: The Gathering* player named Jed McCaleb.

(He had dusted off an old URL he owned at mtgox.com, which he had once used for trading *Magic* cards. In other words, it's an acronym for *Magic: the Gathering* Online Exchange and therefore is pronounced not "Mount Gox" but "Empty Gox".)

McCaleb eventually moved on to other projects, including the banking-focused altcoin known as Ripple, and sold the site to a Japan-based corporation under CEO Mark Karpeles.

Its name proved to be prophetic. In early 2014, Mt Gox was the scene of the worst Bitcoin heist to date. $460 million in bitcoins was stolen by hackers, and millions of dollars more were missing from its bank accounts. It never recovered, and shut down completely later that year.

The newer Ethereum blockchain would not be spared the indignity of being hacked either. Unlike Bitcoin, Ethereum is far more automated. In Chapter Three, we learned how it relies on automated transactions known as 'smart contracts'. An attacker was able to exploit a security weakness to drain a key DAO (known simply as 'The DAO'), draining more than 3.6 million units of ether into a 'child' DAO he had created. Ether's price crashed, and panicked developers tried to stem the flow. You've already seen the result in the chapter on altcoins, but as we speak, the vulnerabilities that led to those attackers have long been patched up.

Don't put anything into an ICO that you can't afford to lose. Hacks don't have to be malicious; sometimes they're the result of simple mistakes. My partners and I have personal experience of this; we helped to fund an ICO for Polkadot, a promising network that aimed to seamlessly link blockchains of various tokens together. It had all the pedigree we could ask for; besides being extraordinarily well-financed, it was led by Ethereum co-founder Dr Gavin Wood himself.

Unfortunately, a programming error in early November 2017 accidentally deleted a critical library of functions, locking in US$150 million in ether! Fortunately, they are still honouring our investment but they lost $150 million worth of ether.

It remains to be seen if Polkadot will recover from such a devastating loss of most of its funds, but the more important principle is that in this field where history is being written, even the best aren't infallible.

Yet remember that *Bitcoin itself, and any altcoin worth its salt, is beyond the ability of anyone to alter by hacking or brute force.* We've already seen that each block in the chain is secured through a cryptographical technique called a 'hash'.

That's not all. Each block carries a 'stamp' of the one before it, so every subsequent block will have to be altered. Tampering with multiple blocks would take more computing power than exists in the world to crack, and it would need billions of years to do so. The universe will probably not last that long, let alone anyone who might benefit.

But crypto is, rightly or wrongly, too tempting a target to give up on. This is why hackers keep trying... and occasionally, they do succeed. How?

What if I told you that most cracking of user accounts is done without ever touching a keyboard? Thanks to Hollywood, the dominant image when you think "hacker" is a pasty faced teenager in a dark bedroom typing furiously—and then a traffic light in the next town goes wonky, or a bank loses thousands of dollars.

The truth is that the vast majority of hacking is done without typing a single line of code. It's actually done on a device a century older, the telephone. And it's fuelled by something older still— human gullibility. In fact, it's basic social engineering, much the same process used to hack bank, email and online shopping accounts, only applied to crypto exchanges.

Think of a soccer game within a foolproof league that cannot be fixed due to the vast sums of money needed. Attacking the process of Bitcoin itself is like fixing the match, something extremely difficult in itself and, if tried, would be impossible to hide.

Anyone looking to score a goal must do it the old-fashioned way, and that's getting the ball past multiple layers of defence. Everyone—forwards, midfielders and defenders—has a part to play, and only after all of those have failed does the goalkeeper come into play.

In this analogy, the hackers are the opposing team, and stopping them requires effort and vigilance on everyone's part. Relying only on your exchange or your telco to step up its game is like demanding your goalkeeper handle the entire defence alone!

Another way of looking at it—an exchange or wallet being hacked due to poor user behaviour or bad code is like the bank being robbed, while hacking the blockchain itself is like printing counterfeit money. But in blockchain, this is something that is very unlikely to happen.

We've already seen that the core architecture of Bitcoin is solid enough. The code resisted every hacking attempt that researcher Dan Kaminsky (the man who famously found a flaw in the Internet itself) threw at it, and its industrial-grade encryption makes it extremely unlikely to be tampered with.

Instead, they target the human element. They scam users and exchange employees careless enough to divulge their keys over the phone or through a phishing site, or extort them from holders of key information via threats to their families or reputations. Those methods have been deployed since the start of banking itself.

Generally, scammers try to get the personal information they need to impersonate their victims, usually on the telephone. They might try:

- *Scam phone calls.* A scammer may claim to be from your bank, and ask for your account number and login information.

- *Phishing emails.* An email might come from scammers impersonating your exchange; they might ask for your login details to repair a made-up 'problem' with your account. Never give your login information to anyone!

Once they have this information, they might call your exchange and try to fool customer support representatives. The brilliance of social engineering comes from the fact that the process is so adaptable. The recon that works on you also works on your telco, your exchange and your bank representative, meaning attackers can try again and again at very little cost. One target had a scammer call his bank six times—the first five reps smelled a rat and refused, only for the sixth to fall for it!

In short, the value of cryptocurrencies makes them a tempting new target for hackers and scammers. Their tools haven't changed much, and so the methods to protect yourself against them aren't new either:

1. Keep only what you need for immediate trading in your exchange, and store the rest 'cold' (that is, offline), preferably in a hardware wallet.

Think of your hardware wallet as a safe. In the same way that money and items in one are secured and taken out of circulation (unless someone with the combination decides otherwise), wallets secure your bitcoins and altcoins offline in a device sealed away from the Internet, until you decide otherwise by plugging it into your computer.

2. Never divulge your user ID and password to anyone, whether via email, a website or over the phone. An actual technical support person will not require this information. If you receive an email threatening that your account will be deleted if you don't access a 'special' site and enter your details, ignore it or contact the organisation itself.

3. Don't open emails or text messages with suspicious links.

4. Use difficult-to-guess usernames and passwords, and secure them with a password manager if needed. Too many people use their own names, their birthdays or other easily-guessed terms.

Computer security has always been an arms race, with increasingly sophisticated tools being deployed on both the attacking and defending sides as time goes on. But even cybersecurity chief Eugene Kaspersky admits:

In the end, I can't shake off a disturbing thought: no matter how great security technologies and measures are, the security of millions can be easily compromised by the oldest threat actor there is—a $5 USB stick and a misguided employee.[4]

The hack of the DAO, and the theft of one-sixth of all the ether in the world, was the result of a weakness within the setup of DAOs and smart contracts themselves. In this case, the hacker knew exactly what he was doing, and the community took swift and decisive action. And because Ethereum is organised differently from Bitcoin, it could be done.

This isn't meant to scare you off Bitcoin or the Net itself, but as a reminder that while new technologies like Ethereum have their teething problems, the fundamentals of protecting yourself never change.

Get secure and media-savvy, and the bad guys will have a much harder time getting to you. Even if they do, the best investors never put in what they can't afford to lose. The best Internet security in the world is still between your ears.

Long story short: You can do your part to prevent crypto theft through good user-end security practices, many of which are already widely known. In Appendix 1, where I share how you can buy your own cryptocurrency, I'll also be recommending a hardware wallet to keep your bitcoins and other tokens safely offline. Industry standards are also being updated to keep service providers (and their employees) accountable, but that doesn't excuse individual users from their responsibility.

So the next time someone tells you crypto is easily stolen, ask them if they know what exactly the thieves do. If they can't answer that question, smile diplomatically and change the subject. (Don't step on toes—you know the saying, you don't know who they might belong to.)

Claim Three: "It's a pyramid scheme—it just benefits early adopters at the expense of everyone else."

I hear this one a lot, even from well-informed people. "In my view, digital currencies are nothing but an unfounded fad (or perhaps even a pyramid scheme), based on a willingness to ascribe value to something that has little or none beyond what people will pay for it," billionaire investor Howard Marks has written.[5]

This one is based on the fact that early investors in Bitcoin own most of them, and can sell their investments at great prices to newcomers with little knowledge of what they're getting into. However, Bitcoin doesn't fit the MO of pyramid schemes, in which those recruited sooner *must* recruit other people themselves to cover their initial investments, with money eventually flowing to the founders at the top of the pyramid.

By definition, a pyramid scheme is centralised so as to have money flowing to a single, central authority 'upline'—something Bitcoin, with its P2P system and inability of even its developers to tamper with it, is not. Even the intervention of Ethereum's creators was done as a result of an unprecedented event, and is unlikely to happen again; and given Ethereum's nature, no one accuses *it* of being a pyramid scheme.

Marks is correct in that bitcoins don't physically exist and have no value beyond what people will pay for them—but the Bitcoin network and the blockchain it is built on are very real programmes run by millions of computers all over the world. Early adopters of bitcoins are simply early adopters, and the network is not set up to give them any special advantage over anyone else—other than the advantage of investing early on, like it is with any other product.

As Michael Hulleman puts it:

> With Bitcoin and most other altcoins, both early adopters and late adopters can have a win-win outcome.
>
> And like the stock market, those who get in on a stock (or in this case, a Bitcoin) early have the most to gain. So in that sense, yes, early adopters who bought in back in 2009 and held onto their cryptocurrency can stand to gain more than late adopters. Bitcoin has made many average people millionaires over the years.[6]

"From a social point of view, Bitcoin is a pure market. The price of Bitcoins fluctuates based on market supply, demand, and perceived value," writes Tiana Laurence, author of *Blockchain for Dummies*.[7]

In other words, early adoption of Bitcoin works the same as it does for any other financial product. The *only* reason why this criticism is made, in my opinion, is because nothing like it has ever existed before.

Claim Four: "It's illegal."

This one is partially true, as Bitcoin is restricted in several countries such as Bangladesh, Bolivia or Nepal. (No book can keep up with the legal specifics, however—a comprehensive list can be found at www.bitcoinbans.com.) However, that in itself is no reason to trade in them elsewhere; otherwise, coin exchanges wouldn't exist. Bitcoin and cryptos in general actually have the *blessing* of governments worldwide—and as we'll see in the next chapter, it's not for want of power to tamper with them.

Some people point to the arrest of Mt Gox CEO Mark Karpeles, but this is the arrest of a Bitcoin exchange leader, not a developer of Bitcoin itself. That said, the 'anonymous' nature of cryptocurrencies is enough to bring us to...

Claim Five: "It's anonymous and a boon for criminals. I don't want to be a criminal."

This sounds plausible—for some people, the first they've heard of Bitcoin was through some big incident, such as the aforementioned hacks, the illegal Silk Road marketplace or the WannaCry attack on computers all over the world; the latter two involved payment in Bitcoin. Because cryptocurrencies transact between pseudonymous *addresses*, rather than *people*, the dominant idea seems to be one of a shady, untraceable scheme that no respectable person would want to be a part of.

Pseudonymity Explained

I'd like to explain a little more about the claim that Bitcoin and other cryptocurrencies are somehow 'anonymous'. Perhaps the prefix 'crypto' is partially to blame—it brings up images of spies, coded messages and hidden, cloak-and-dagger deals.

Let's recall what happens when a miner verifies a transaction added to Bitcoin's publicly-available blockchain. The only record anyone can see is that nonsense address A sent X bitcoins to nonsense address B. But *both* addresses, and their full transactions histories, are publicly available. This means that anyone you send bitcoins effectively knows the entire history of the address you did it with—be it gambling, purchases you'd rather keep private, or charitable and political causes.

It is true that your wallet doesn't have your name associated with it. "While it is possible to create a wallet and never associate your true identity to it, one could follow the money to discover the identity of a wallet holder," writes Hulleman. "This is possible because exchanges where you can purchase a cryptocurrency with fiat have identification requirements to ensure that you're not a criminal."[8]

"Blockchain is open, and everyone sees everything. Thus, blockchain has no real anonymity. It offers pseudonymity instead," says Kaspersky Lab's Alexey Malanov. It gets worse for companies:

> All of their contracting parties, sales, customers, account amounts, and every other little, petty detail would all become public. Financial transparency is perhaps one of the largest disadvantages of using Bitcoin.[9]

Indeed, guess what's even *more* untraceable than crypto? Good old cash, which criminals have been using since money replaced barter trading. After all, who knows the transaction history of that S$50 note in your wallet? It could've been used to pay a taxi driver one day, traded for goods the next, used to pay a drug dealer the next, and so on.

There's no way to tell, though it does provide a great reason to wash your hands every time you handle money.

Pseudonymity just means that your crypto address functions like your email. There's no reason compelling you to create an email address in your own name, so you can choose the name you'd like to go by when you sign up with say, Gmail. But there *is* identifiable information that can be used to conclusively identify the country you're surfing from, your Internet service provider and eventually you personally, given enough resources.

As far as Bitcoin is concerned, nothing could be further from the truth. Bitcoin's blockchain is built not on secrecy, but transparency. Every transaction from Nakamoto's Genesis Block to that payment for a Starbucks soy latte a second ago is on public record. The only information not readily available is who paid whom, but even that can be found out with enough time; after all, the FBI was able to track down Silk Road founder Ross Ulbrecht through his IP address, down to the very library stack he was in.

Others point to arrests of key figures in the Bitcoin world. As journalist Kyle Torpey writes at the Nasdaq website about the failure of Silk Road and Mt Gox:

The inability to make the distinction between Bitcoin and the companies or services built on top of it has been a huge problem for the digital currency in terms of education. Because of this inability to distinguish between Bitcoin and Bitcoin companies, many people thought the CEO of Bitcoin had been arrested [...] Of course, the reality is that there is no CEO of Bitcoin.[10]

Note that while those *operations* were illegal, the *medium of exchange* they used were not. The bitcoins seized from Ulbrecht were ultimately sold at auction by the US government, with portions bought up by parties like Tim Draper and Chicago-based trading firm DRW—both early adopters of Bitcoin. It is noted that the latter bought 27,000 bitcoins worth $7.6 million, a holding worth over $300 million as of this writing.[11]

Some cryptocurrencies are gaining favour among criminals, such as the altcoin called Monero—which we've seen encrypts addresses and obscures the identity of senders and recipients. But in the same way that a firearm can be used by both a policeman and a terrorist, that doesn't make them all boons for criminal activity. As *Wealth Advisor* notes:

> Developers behind Monero say they simply created a coin that protects privacy. Most people use it legitimately—they just don't want others to know whether they're buying a coffee or a car, Riccardo Spagni, core developer at Monero, said in a phone interview. "As a community, we certainly don't advocate for Monero's use by criminals," Spagni said. "At the same time if you have a decentralised currency, it's not like you can prevent someone from using it. I imagine that Monero provides massive advantages for criminals over Bitcoin, so they would use Monero."[12]

At day's end, blockchain and cryptocurrencies are simply tools. Their effect comes down to the intent of the user.

Claim Six: "There'll just be a bubble. It's too volatile to ever be a viable financial product."
Counter anyone who tells you this by asking how much Bitcoin has appreciated over the last five years. It's true that prices have fluctuated and even plunged as banks and governments tried to figure out what to do, most notably during China's temporary ban of domestic crypto trading.

But there're two things to note. First, the trajectory of Bitcoin, Ether and other key cryptocurrencies have remained on the uptrend. We've already seen that 10,000 bitcoins could've bought you a pizza in 2010; just seven years later, that amount could retire you for life.

Second, a bubble won't mean the end of the crypto world. As anyone who tracks cryptocurrency prices will tell you, Bitcoin, Ether and many other cryptos have seen great ups and downs. Even if they *are* a bubble, people only speak of the failures... and never the successes that result. But Clem Chambers writes at *Forbes*:

> Bubble markets look the same, be they dotcom bubbles, single stock bubbles or Bitcoin. They go up like a rocket and come down like a rock. However, the point I was making was that massive companies will come out of these emergent technologies, companies like Amazon, which came out of the dotcom crash. The children of the cryptocurrency bubble will be colossal.[13]

In other words, bubbles don't end industries; they shake them up so that whoever innovates and thrives in the end will be far larger and more stable than before. (Even the classic Dutch 'tulip mania' bust didn't last, and by some accounts its impact has been greatly exaggerated.[14] Tulips remain a booming, billion-dollar industry in Holland to this day.) The dotcom bubble threw up dozens of social networking sites like MySpace and Friendster, but the final winner picking up all the chips turned out to be the multibillion-dollar Facebook.

How bubbles end matters, but they don't have to affect your profit and loss. Just like games, all bubbles have winners and losers, and great gains have been made along the way.

I'm not alone in pointing this out. Graticule Asset Management Asia's CIO Adam Levinson does so in the Foreword to this book, and so does my former boss at Tudor Investment Corp, Paul Tudor Jones. The "plot" of today's market, he notes, is "much the same today but we can substitute Bitcoin and fine art for the Nasdaq 100 of 1999."[15]

Cryptos are simply going through, at an accelerated pace, the same iterative cycle that all new technologies, companies and stocks must. Nothing is happening here that is unique to them, and it's possible that much of the uncertainty comes from the fact that cryptocurrencies are the first truly new invention in living memory.

Even then, I urge cautious optimism—again, just because you can use bitcoins for daily transactions, it doesn't mean you should. Only time will tell if the SegWit measure (and the hard fork that created Bitcoin Cash) will truly take care of the rise in transaction fees. Until things stabilise to affordable levels that both miners and customers are happy with, most experts recommend treating it like they would any other asset, simply holding as much as possible and letting it grow. If you must spend it day-to-day, use another crypto with lower transaction rates, such as Litecoin.

"Cryptocurrencies are not a normal investment," warns BlockGeeks. "The volatility grossly exceeds that of any other investment class. It is to some parts unregulated. There is the risk that cryptocurrencies get outlawed, that exchanges get hacked or that you lose your cryptocurrency key. Cryptocurrencies are a high-risk investment."[16]

Bitcoin's greatest rival isn't another crypto, but its own success and limitations. How well it handles those will determine its worth in the future. As we've seen, the prime movers have already had to implement the drastic solution of spinning off a new version of themselves. Just like any new technology, there'll always be teething problems as its pioneers explore uncharted territory. Remember it's about getting rich, not getting it right.

Generally, this is true of ideas being tested for the first time, and the pioneering cryptos are effectively working out solutions to problems so their successors won't have to reinvent the wheel.

My suggestion for this phase of crypto's growth is to keep as much crypto as you can as assets—again, just because you can pay for purchases in Bitcoin, it doesn't mean you should. Because they resemble stocks more than they do liquid cash, it's better to treat them as such. Some cryptos such as Litecoin are designed for this, so feel free to experiment.

That's why crypto is unlikely to wipe fiat currency off the map like digital cameras did to traditional film. Precisely because central banks keep fiat currencies stable, they are more suitable for your immediate needs and will stay that way for the near future. (Appendix 3 lists my favourite places to get the news if, and when, that ever changes.)

Your New Blocks

- Cryptos are similar to other financial products in that they are stores of value.
- Take the precautions to secure your bitcoins and other crypto holdings, and you will not have to worry about the vast majority of hacks.
- Crypto is pseudonymous, not anonymous; it's actually less useful for criminals than cash.
- Crypto is legal in most countries, and can serve as a reserve store of value in most of the world. However, exchanges and ICOs are subject to government regulation.
- Crypto's volatility stems from its present role as an untested new technology, and should stabilise with time.

Notes

[1] Quoted in Pete Rizzo, "Warren Buffett Urges Investors to 'Stay Away' from Bitcoin," *Coindesk*, 14 March 2014, at https://www.coindesk.com/warren-buffett-investors-stay-away-bitcoin.

[2] Michael Hulleman, "10 Bitcoin Scams, Criticisms, and Myths Explained," *Hobo with a Laptop*, 10 August 2017, at https://hobowithalaptop.com/bitcoin-scams-myths-criticisms.

[3] Today you can visit the Hole in the Wall, a hideout in the mountains of Wyoming where the great outlaws of the nineteenth century hid from authorities hunting them.

[4] Eugene Kaspersky, "We aggressively protect our users and we're proud of it," *Kaspersky Lab*, 5 October 2017, at https://eugene.kaspersky.com/2017/10/05/we-aggressively-protect-our-users-and-were-proud-of-it.

[5] Quoted in Madeline Farber, "This Billionaire Just Called Bitcoin a 'Pyramid Scheme'," Fortune, 27 July 2017, at http://fortune.com/2017/07/27/howard-marks-bitcoin-pyramid-scheme.

[6] Michael Hulleman, "10 Bitcoin Scams, Criticisms, and Myths Explained," Hobo with a Laptop, 10 August 2017, at https://hobowithalaptop.com/bitcoin-scams-myths-criticisms.

[7] Tiana Laurence, "Debunking Some Common Bitcoin Misconceptions," Dummies. com, (no date), at http://www.dummies.com/personal-finance/debunking-common-bitcoin-misconceptions.

[8] Michael Hulleman, "10 Bitcoin Scams, Criticisms, and Myths Explained," Hobo with a Laptop, 10 August 2017, at https://hobowithalaptop.com/bitcoin-scams-myths-criticisms.

[9] Alexey Malanov, "Six myths about blockchain and Bitcoin: Debunking the effectiveness of the technology," Kaspersky Lab, 18 August 2017, at https://www.kaspersky.com/blog/bitcoin-blockchain-issues/18019.

[10] Kyle Torpey, "Top 10 Myths About Bitcoin," Nasdaq, 13 May 2016, at http://www.nasdaq. com/article/top-10-myths-about-bitcoin-cm620562.

[11] Sterlin Lujan, "DRW and Other Firms Embrace High-Frequency Bitcoin Trading," Bitcoin News, 23 October 2017, at https://news.bitcoin.com/drw-and-other-firms-embrace-high-frequency-bitcoin-trading.

[12] Bloomberg, "The Criminal Underworld Is Dropping Bitcoin for Another Currency," Wealth Advisor, 2 January 2018, at https://www.thewealthadvisor.com/article/criminal-underworld-dropping-bitcoin-another-currency.

[13] Clem Chambers, "Cryptocurrency Is A Bubble, Revisited," Forbes, 8 August 2017, at https://www.forbes.com/sites/investor/2017/08/08/cryptocurrency-is-a-bubble-revisited/#46e8f3613f0a.

[14] For more, see: Lorraine Boissoneault, "There Never Was a Real Tulip Fever," The Smithsonian, 18 September 2017, at https://www.smithsonianmag.com/history/there-never-was-real-tulip-fever-180964915.

[15] Tyler Durden, "Paul Tudor Jones: "This Market, Which Is Reminiscent Of The 1999 Bubble, Is On The Verge Of A Significant Change," Zero Hedge, 3 December 2017, at https://www.zerohedge.com/news/2017-12-03/paul-tudor-jones-market-which-reminiscent-1999-bubble-verge-significant-change.

[16] "How to Invest in Cryptocurrencies: Ultimate Guide," BlockGeeks, (no date), at https:// blockgeeks.com/guides/how-to-invest-in-cryptocurrencies

CHAPTER 7

HOLD YOUR HORSES

> Many will find this crazy, but I think bitcoin could surpass
> the dollar as reserve currency within the next 10-15 years.
>
> —Brian Armstrong, CEO of Coinbase[1]

If there's an obvious flaw in Bitcoin's community, it's the way its champions preach about it. Heck, the only thing missing is the hellfire-and-brimstone part, and Bitcoin's proponents have that covered by creating *FOMO* and threatening that you're missing out on the Next Big Thing.

As powerful, innovative and truly international as Bitcoin (and crypto in general) is, there remain issues you need to be aware of—and the more bitcoins you hold, the more careful you need to be. A number of unrealistic expectations have grown up around Bitcoin, and I encourage you to look at them with a healthy scepticism.

Here are the biggest claims made about Bitcoin (and crypto in general) that need to be taken with more than a few grains of salt.

Claim One: Blockchains are immutable, and a 51 percent attack is logistically impossible.
It may look like I'm taking aim at a sacred cow, but I'm actually

more in favour of taking down bad ideas before they become too big to question.

Bitcoin's proponents, including many political libertarians, cite the network's cryptographic protection, the sheer number of nodes and the need to take over more than half the computing power of the network—the so-called '51 percent attack' needed to place every transaction in the world under any one party. (For how this would work see Chapter Two, where I discuss the fifth part of Satoshi Nakamoto's abstract.)

Such a herculean effort, they tell us, would be out of anyone's reach. As Tiana Laurence puts it: "In order to pull this off, an attacker would need the equivalent of all the energy production of Ireland."[2]

Or is it? Dr Gideon Greenspan of Coin Sciences disagrees—it's only because no one rich and powerful enough (and there are plenty of such parties) has actually tried tampering with Bitcoin itself. "In blockchains, there is no such thing as perfect immutability," he says. "The real question is: What are the conditions under which a particular blockchain can and cannot be changed? And do those conditions match the problem we're trying to solve?"[3]

Every blockchain needs validators to ensure that new blocks are added in accordance with the rules. Bitcoin fills this role with its miners, while a private blockchain belonging to a single organisation must do so through their IT administrators or key executives. We've already seen one case of blockchain immutability being blown wide open—the 2016 'rollback' of Ethereum in the wake of the DAO hack.

Greenspan also calculates the actual cost of performing one of Nakamoto's feared '51 percent attacks' on Bitcoin itself. With

US$400 million, one could buy enough mining rigs to match Bitcoin's entire mining capacity... and this sum, while enormous, is easily within the reach of the government of a mid-sized country.

He continues:

> Now think about the reports that Bitcoin is being used by Chinese citizens to circumvent their country's capital controls. And consider further that the Chinese government's tax revenues are approximately $3 trillion per year. Would a non-democratic country's government spend 0.04% of its budget to shut down a popular method for illegally taking money out of that country? I wouldn't claim that the answer is necessarily yes. But if you think the answer is definitely no, you're being more than a little naive.[4]

But the Chinese government could tamper with Bitcoin much more easily than this. According to many reliable estimates, 80% of Bitcoin mining is done in China and therefore within the ability of the Chinese military to strong-arm into censoring or invalidating any transaction they wanted.

Is such an attack therefore possible? Yes. Is it probable? No, but China keeps its hands off Bitcoin's architecture not because it can't interfere, but because it chooses not to.

Immutability, then, is relative and depends on who needs the blockchain adjusted. As Greenspan says:

> The Bitcoin blockchain and its ilk are not immutable in any perfect or absolute sense. Rather, they are immutable

so long as nobody big enough and rich enough decides to destroy them. Still, by relying on the economic cost of subverting the network, cryptocurrency immutability satisfies the specific needs of people who don't want to trust governments, companies and banks. It may not be perfect, but it's the best they can do.[5]

Like it or not, there's no escaping Caesar's wrath, should he decide to execute it... although we've also seen that it may not be in his best interests to do so. Bitcoin may not have this vulnerability given how popular it is; but can the same be said for smaller coins like Zcash, Golem or Monero?

Claim Two: Cryptos will replace traditional currency; there'll never be a need to use fiat money again.
No, they won't. They have too many inefficiencies built in by design—because miners compete to approve transactions, it takes time to approve even the smallest transaction, and even then it may sit in a queue for hours without going through if the attached transaction fee is too low to attract miners' notice. And as we saw in the chapter on altcoins, it will take time to work out the kinks that prevent the blockchain from having the scalability it needs.

"Given the transaction-processing speed, significantly increasing the number of active users simply isn't possible," observes Malanov. "For comparison, Visa processes thousands of transactions per second and, if required, can easily increase its bandwidth. After all, classic banking technologies are scalable."[6]

Will Crypto Catch Up?

Granted, cryptocurrency developers are working to replicate this. For instance, a protocol known as the Lightning Network aims to set up instant transactions in Bitcoin, and Dash uses a method called InstantSend. How it works is beyond the scope of this book, but you can read a basic explanation at CoinCenter.[7]

Bitcoin is here to stay, but in its current form it's unlikely to replace fiat currency. That said, anything can still happen, and none other than Draper remains optimistic. "In five years, if you go to a Starbucks or McDonald's and try to buy a burger or coffee with fiat currency, the person at the counter is going to laugh at you," he told delegates at San Francisco's Blockchain Connect Conference in January 2018. The current volatility and technical issues that cryptocurrencies face, he says, are "fits and starts" that will be corrected over time.[8]

In conclusion, what should we make of crypto, given the arguments for and against it? One side sees in it the end of the state, when economies break free of the governments that control them; the other sees an anarchic Wild West vulnerable to hackers, criminals and scammers out to prey on the innocent.

I hope this chapter has given you a sober look at both sides, and shown that the truth is more complicated than that. Yes, blockchain is an evolving new technology with many uses in the financial and tech world that remain to be seen. Yes, Bitcoin is opening up new possibilities that governments will keep playing catch-up with.

But it's unlikely to utterly kill the need for trusted institutions. After all, to most ordinary people who don't care how it works and don't want to wait hours for some miner to approve their transaction, cash remains the order of the day.

Your New Blocks

- Crypto isn't immutable in an absolute sense, and comes with significant drawbacks that have yet to be overcome.
- Be cautiously optimistic about its future; it's here to stay, and with its track record, you can be confident of it as a financial product and store of value, if not a replacement for fiat money.

Notes

[1] Tweet by Brian Armstrong, 23 July 2015, at https://twitter.com/brian_armstrong/ status/624422827307831296.

[2] Tiana Laurence, "Debunking Some Common Bitcoin Misconceptions," *Dummies. com*, (no date), at http://www.dummies.com/personal-finance/debunking-common-bitcoin-misconceptions.

[3] Gideon Greenspan, "The Blockchain Immutability Myth," *LinkedIn*, 4 May 2017, at https:// www.linkedin.com/pulse/blockchain-immutability-muth-gideon-greenspan.

[4] Ibid.

[5] Ibid.

[6] Alexey Malanov, "Six myths about blockchain and Bitcoin: Debunking the effectiveness of the technology," *Kaspersky Lab*, 18 August 2017, at https://www.kaspersky.com/blog/bitcoin-blockchain-issues/18019.

[7] Elizabeth Stark, "What is the Lightning Network and how can it help Bitcoin scale?" *CoinCentre*, 15 September 2016, at https://coincenter.org/entry/what-is-the-lightning-network.

[8] Quoted in Ari Levy, "Burgers and coffee will all be bought with cryptocurrency in five years, said Tim Draper," *CNBC*, 26 January 2018, at https://www.cnbc.com/2018/01/26/tim-draper-burgers-and-coffee-will-be-bought-with-crypto-in-5-years.html.

"IS THIS A HARD TRADE?"

> Scientists are the enemies of tradition. And tradition owns all the prisons.
>
> —Eoin Colfer, *Airman*

I grew up in Kuala Lumpur's Bukit Bintang, in a ghetto called Roundmouth. My parents were separated when I was little, so I was the only child—my brothers and sisters were the friends I made on the street.

At an early age, I realised that value was found in what people wanted, and traded for. That in itself was a kind of *currency*—we bartered soda bottle caps, decorated ice cream sticks, playing cards and marbles. That was my first concept of money, as something with an agreed value that you could trade for things you wanted.

On my daily walk to school along some eerily quiet routes, I have also been robbed and extorted of my lunch money. That brought home a lesson—that because money is valuable, some people will do whatever it takes to get it. **Just like coins in exchanges can be hacked, fiat money can be taken away.**

This is a centralised world. Roundmouth was a close community centred on a food centre known as a *cjar dhong* (茶档)", where I helped out in the fried rice stall, and also sold sugar cane drinks after school. Some regulars didn't even pay for their food—they had credit lines where they wrote what they owed in small 555 notebooks kept by the vendor. Once such a notebook got lost; that painful lesson got some of them to distribute the records. **Having two identical notebooks is the first breakthrough of data being distributed.**

I would later learn they were called 'ledgers' in accounting class in England, where I went to pursue my dream of being a chartered accountant. Before my first paycheck from Deutsche Bank, the Malaysian ringgit depreciated 75% against the British pound—and I learned that rare commodities would still hold their value, such as gold and rare stamps. This also shows that ledgers and fiat money can depreciate 75% in a short time. **So, volatility of crypto is not unique.**

I landed a permanent post on the FX trading desk in London at the time the industry was busy transitioning to the euro. The bank sent me to its Thai office, then to Singapore in 2000, during which my focus turned to shor-term interest rate trading. Subsequently I moved to JPMorgan Chase and ABN AMRO before returning to London with Goldman Sachs in 2007, at the peak of the financial froth.

In financial turmoils, money can disappear and even property prices can double in a short time. Being in one of the busiest trading floors in the world, I was in the middle of some of the most frantic financial action ever; I traded in markets where bids offers suddenly disappeared, with people making and losing lots of money in just a few minutes. What I learned was that markets can overrun and correct (that is, sharply retrace that recent change), but an underlying trend prevails. **Execution and risk management**

became the most important skills to have. Trading crypto is the same.

I moved to Hong Kong in 2010 with Goldman Sachs, in a year when property prices almost doubled—and again, precious commodities rose in value. Next, I returned to Singapore to join Tudor Investment Corp as a portfolio manager.

It was a dream come true to work for someone I read about as a legend when I was younger. Through Paul Tudor Jones and all my friends there, I learned what execution and risk management in trading really mean. One of the favourite questions Paul would ask me (and probably himself) was: "Is this a hard trade?"

After five years managing money in Tudor, my tech dreams started. I co-founded a few tech startups, including Shentilium, a spinoff from a National University of Singapore project. That was my entry into blockchain, and the vast new opportunities that opened up.

Crypto is today in that grey area between full-fledged revolution and flash in the pan fad, but if history is any witness, it's telling us that one very powerful genie is out of the bottle, and there's no putting it back in.

Whose Genie Is This?

Who then controls the genie? Who has the power to turn it to good and not to evil, and determines whether it succeeds or fails in its wish-granting? The answer, just as it has always been with history, is its end-users. It's you, and it's me. It will grow as more uses are found for it, and more users buy in with their wallets and choices.

Will it replace conventional money? Not in the near future, even if some steps are being taken in that direction. Like it or not, there will always be people who prefer the reliability of fiat money, and who at present may not fancy waiting an hour for some miner somewhere to approve their payment for a meal.

At the same time, Bitcoin and its ecosystem of competitors *will* form a reserve currency of sorts. Remember JPMorgan Chase CEO Jamie Dimon's comments at the beginning of this book?

Dominic Frisby observes:

> Although JPMorgan was by no means the most leveraged of the banks, it still took bailout money, and, as its CEO, Dimon and Bitcoin will inevitably be philosophically opposed. His utter faith in the US dollar sounds rather like the boss of a major record label talking up CDs a year before the iPod was brought to market.[1]

It isn't so hard to work out where I stand either, and I'm in very good company. Yes, crypto still has teething problems to work out. Yes, its exchanges remain vulnerable to hackers, scammers and other lowlifes. Yes, it faces scalability issues and may change to comply with new laws and regulations. All of these will happen as long as it's human beings who gather, store and use it. But as a form of decentralised stored value that allows anyone with an Internet connection to participate, it has no equal.

If you've read this far, you're now better equipped than most people when it comes to cryptocurrencies as a financial product, store of value and—should you choose to use it as such—spendable money. All the same, when gathering it for yourself, ask yourself the same question that Paul does: "Is this a hard trade?" I hope I've helped you answer that question.

Thanks for joining me on this journey through the wild, wild world of cryptocurrency. You now know enough to make your own decisions concerning it, and hopefully you'll find it as exciting a development as I have.

Notes

[1] Dominic Frisby, "Don't let the bankers fool you: bitcoin is here to stay," *The Guardian*, 15 September 2017, at https://www.theguardian.com/commentisfree/2017/sep/15/jp-morgan-ceo-wrong-bitcoin-jamie-dimon.

APPENDIX 1

COUNT ME IN: GETTING STARTED WITH CRYPTO

> I always tell them [my family] that the second most stupid thing they could do right now is to own an amount of bitcoins they cannot afford to lose and the most stupid thing they could do would be to not own any.
>
> —Wences Casares, CEO of Xapo[1]

In this appendix, you'll see:
- How to buy your own cryptocurrency
- What crypto exchanges do
- How to securely store it so it's safe from hackers

Now you know how bitcoins work, it's time to get your very own stash to keep. Their value is likely to increase over time, like a well-chosen stock, even if there are shorter-term rises and falls. Prices, as we learn in financial trading, tend to move in waves.

Note that cryptocurrencies don't face many of the regulations that traditional currencies or equities do, so their value is much more vulnerable to speculation and other forms of investor behaviour; but as Bitcoin has shown, they can be a great investment opportunity if combined with other products. Remember, the old rules still apply, such as not keeping all your eggs in one basket.

This section will get you up and running as a new crypto owner, then introduce some of the basic concepts of trading and buying new altcoins to expand your portfolio. (In Chapter Five, we saw what altcoins are and why there are hundreds of them around.)

Acquiring Your First Bitcoins

How do you jump on the crypto bandwagon? Fortunately, it's far less complicated than it would seem at first.

There are four ways you can receive crypto:

- You can buy it with fiat money from a crypto trading firm, or *exchange*.

- You can buy it directly from other owners, or via a brokerage.

- You can be paid in it for a good or service, like you would fiat money.

- You can mine it using your computer. (Mining bitcoins, given the competition, isn't recommended; coins only go to the first computer that breaks the encryption on a given block, and with a single home-based setup, it's very unlikely yours will win that race.)

Unlike other financial products, they can be bought in just a few minutes, with nothing more complex than your credit card or a PayPal account.

Getting started with crypto is as simple as opening an account with a crypto exchange like Coinbase. (Bear in mind, however, that not all exchanges operate in all countries.) Once you find one that does, you can buy as much as you're willing to.

Exchanges can and have been hacked; because of the sheer amount of money that exchanges handle, they're evergreen targets for hackers. Because the rewards are so vast, they're willing to invest much time and effort finding vulnerabilities. Size is no protection; just ask the now-former leaders of ex-industry champion Mt Gox, which lost millions of dollars' worth of bitcoins in one of the most infamous hacks ever. But by and large, security across the industry is improving, and wallet-users have far less to worry about.

Here are the basic steps of getting some of your very own bitcoins from the Web into your wallet:

Optional prep step: Get a secure means of storing your bitcoins once you have them. This might take the form of a paper or hardware 'wallet'. Paper wallets are slips of paper with a printed QR code; when scanned, it will take you to your crypto storage. Hardware wallets are a step further—they're essentially USB sticks that store the credentials you need to access your crypto.

While a wallet isn't needed to buy your first crypto tokens, when you have a sizeable amount it becomes a no-brainer to get one for the additional security.

Step 1: Take your time to research the cryptocurrency exchanges that can operate in your country and that accept the payment options available to you.

"Remember that purchasing cryptocurrencies with a credit card will always require identity verification and come with a premium price as there is a higher risk of fraud and higher transaction and processing fees," says the cryptocurrencies purchasing guide at BlockGeeks. "Purchasing cryptocurrency via wire transfer will take significantly longer as it takes time for banks to process."[2]

For the purposes of this book, I recommend starting with Coinbase, then experimenting with other exchanges as you go along.

Step 2: Open a new Coinbase account at www.coinbase.com. Enter your particulars, including your name, email address and phone number for two-factor authentication, or 2FA. (Note that even 2FA isn't completely foolproof; exchanges might have updated their security precautions by the time you read this.)

You'll be assigned a Bitcoin address, a string of letters and numbers that represents your identity; it works like an email address, except this is for sending and receiving crypto tokens.

Step 3: Decide how much you're going to buy. This varies based on your financial state and appetite for risk; again, never invest what you're unable to lose. When you're ready, click 'Buy', and select the number of bitcoins available for your budget.

Most people will initially trade in small fractions of a bitcoin, given that a full bitcoin costs thousands of US dollars. The smallest tradeable unit is a hundred millionth of a bitcoin, named a *satoshi* in honour of its creator.

Step 4: Transfer your new coins to your wallet. The exact steps may differ depending on your wallet's design and vendor, but the result is the same; your Bitcoin address is linked to the wallet, making that wallet the only way anyone in the world can access it.

What's next? Try buying other coins on the same site, using the less important ones as an experiment before trading some of those hard-bought bitcoins.

At *Forbes*, Clem Chambers suggests treating crypto trading like a game. Start with smaller coins as a kind of practice mode; that way, if you misapply the principles, the consequences won't be so bad.

"You could play a minnow like Boatcoin or Feathercoin, where $10 of coin gets you a long way, yet their markets can be traded like any stock," he writes.

> For the cost of a Big Mac I've played 'market maker' on these coins. You can 'market make' coins like these like a Wall Street firm and push them around and bully them like a 'white shoe' firm would a Nasdaq stock.[3]

As mentioned in Chapter Seven of this book, I don't recommend using Bitcoin for smaller, day-to-day expenses, despite the number of businesses accepting it. It makes more sense to hold it like a stock—secure in the knowledge that you're holding a piece of technological history, and its value is likely to grow over time.

All the best!

Notes

[1] From an AMA at forum.bitcoin.com, 3 November 2015, at https://forum.bitcoin.com/ama-ask-me-anything/i-am-wences-casares-co-founder-ceo-of-xapo-ask-me-anything-t2025-30.html.

[2] "Best Cryptocurrency Exchanges: The Ultimate Guide," *BlockGeeks*, (no date), at https:// blockgeeks.com/guides/best-cryptocurrency-exchanges.

[3] Clem Chambers, "Cryptocurrency is a Bubble, Revisited," *Forbes*, 8 August 2017, at https:// www.forbes.com/sites/investor/2017/08/08/cryptocurrency-is-a-bubble-revisited

BUILDING THE CRYPTO MINDSET : AN INTERVIEW WITH MELONPORT CEO MONA EL ISA

Mona El Isa hails from Switzerland and was my colleague at Goldman Sachs. She became one of its star traders, reaching the position of Vice President at the age of 26. In 2011 she moved on to Jabre Capital in Geneva, before leaving in 2014 to start her own blockchain software firm, Melonport. Today, she serves as its CEO.

At a recent catch-up, we discussed the future of cryptocurrency as a financial asset; the thinking behind cryptocurrency startups and what they're looking for; and what it takes to become a pioneer in this new and growing field.

Where did the idea of Melonport come from?
Melon is 'future' in Greek, and comes from *melo*, or 'destined to be'. It felt like the portfolio management industry was destined for more modern technology, after having been underpinned by such archaic systems and processes.

I was motivated to co-found Melonport in 2015 after I had experienced first-hand how hard it was to set up and manage a hedge fund with under $200 million in assets under management (AUM). One thing the experience did teach me, though, was how the engine of a fund worked—which I had always been oblivious to, having worked at larger institutions and funds. That 'engine' ran in the background, thanks to the scale these companies had. It is not uncommon for a medium sized hedge-fund to have three or four support staff for every investment professional in order to run the engine.

The idea to use smart contracts to create a decentralised asset management protocol was being discussed back then by visionary Donald McIntyre (Etherplan) and our competitor at the time; Iconomi. Iconomi since abandoned the decentralised vision in favour of centralised asset management and Donald McIntyre went on to change his business plan but he will always be someone who I will respect for his early vision and ideas before anyone else was talking about blockchain and asset managmenet. I saw smart contracts for their ability to modernise and automate a lot of these 'old engine' manual processes, and enforce their behaviour using an entirely 'new engine'—blockchain technology. It was genius! I instinctively felt that this is what the industry needed, and wanted to enable it to happen.

How did you recruit a tech team that knew how to make it work?
We had two criteria when recruiting. First, our team members had to be sponge-like, continuously teaching themselves new things.

Often, Reto would give them a tough technical challenge in a field they knew nothing about. If their attitude was, "I don't know how to code in this language," they were out. If it was, "I don't know about this, but I'll teach myself based on what little information is out there," they had exactly the kind of personality we wanted. If candidates passed the challenge, it was just a question of whether their values aligned with ours.

Second, we look for excellence, passion, love in what they do, and high integrity. We didn't worry too much about diversity; our belief was that it would come naturally, and it did.

Given your experience as a trader at Goldman Sachs, what type of cryptocurrencies do you look for to trade?
I think it's difficult to compare this with anything I ever traded at Goldman. There were real companies and cash flows behind the equities I traded back then. I started off trading Metal and Mining stocks, which were highly volatile in the years before China really took off. So in a way, I'm used to volatility and it doesn't faze me much.

However, cryptocurrencies are experimental technologies— they are unproven and new, and therefore I mainly look at the people behind them. If they are hardworking, adhere to certain values and produce results, then I'm interested... but always with the view that they could easily be worth nothing one day.

Until the market matures, it is important to understand that by investing in cryptocurrencies, you are investing in innovation first and foremost. The value will be linked to the quality of the technology and user adoption. In most cases, it's too early to see evidence of those at this early stage—which makes it very risky. It's important to understand that.

How do you entrust people to invest in cryptocurrencies for you; that is, who plays the role of 'private banker' in the crypto world?

Not many, although there are a few new players trying. Falcon Bank and Bitcoin Suisse in Switzerland were one of the first movers in this vein—and more recently, Bank Frick. There will no doubt be others to come.

What do you have to say to people who deem cryptocurrencies too volatile to be a viable financial product?

Fair enough. Each person should understand what their threshold for volatility is and respect that. Cryptocurrencies may not stay this volatile forever—they are still a very new asset class. As the asset class matures, volatility should come down and one day these same people may feel more comfortable re-considering their view.

Do you think cryptocurrencies will be regarded as a must-have component of an investment portfolio in the future?

Yes! As an example, I like to remind people that 40 years ago junk bonds were seen as 'uninvestable' until Mike Milken came along and pioneered investment in the space.[1] Today it's worth over $40 trillion and most funds have to have some junk bonds as part of their portfolio allocation.

Around the same time, ETFs were also seen as uninvestable, until John Bogle came along and pioneered the way in that. While I still hear people call them uninvestable today, yet there's still a multi-trillion dollar market in them and most investment portfolios have some exposure. I'd even argue that commodities and emerging markets were seen this way—until Goldman Sachs created the GSCI index and Templeton set up the first Emerging Markets fund. Both of these moves pioneered investments into these asset classes too.

Crypto is today's new asset class! It's just not clear who will be the pioneer in it. Some names that come to mind are GABI (Global Advisors) who were the first ever Bitcoin fund out of Jersey, Cyber Fund and Polychain Capital. Those are the earliest cryptocurrency funds I can think of, but it still remains to be seen.

Let's say I have US$10,000 to invest. What's the process of turning that into crypto?

You would open an account with an exchange like Kraken or Bittrex, then transfer money into your account and purchase a cryptocurrency that trades on one of those exchanges. After that, you would be wise to transfer your cryptocurrencies into a secure wallet which you generate, and keep hold of the private key.

Most of the hacks that happen in cryptocurrencies happen on exchanges. So as long as you trust yourself to manage a wallet securely and hold the private key safely, you would be better off storing it securely off the exchange.

A new type of exchange is emerging—decentralised exchanges. These are interesting peer-to-peer exchanges with no middleman involved, only a smart contract. They haven't taken off with huge volumes yet, but they do look promising for the future. If they work, they could possibly be a lot more secure than the exchanges we use today.

Any advice for people new to cryptocurrencies?

If you don't have time to do your homework, don't get involved. As more and more crypto funds emerge, I would look towards experienced managers who have a combination of investment and technology experience, and who dedicate themselves full-time to researching this industry to get some exposure. Only put in what you are prepared to lose, and be honest with yourself about what that number is.

Notes

[1] For more on Milken, see: William D Cohan, "Michael Milken invented the modern junk bond, went to prison, and then became one of the most respected people on Wall Street," *Business Insider*, 2 May 2017, at http://www.businessinsider.com/michael-milken-life-story-2017-5/?IR=T.

WHERE TO GET CAUGHT UP WITH CRYPTO NEWS

Cryptocurrencies in general, and Bitcoin in particular, are in the midst of teething pains. By the time you read this, many of the specifics will definitely be out of date. No book can keep up with the changes to Bitcoin alone... to say nothing of the thousands of cryptos in circulation.

Of course, Google is a big help. But I prefer to read people I trust to deliver great content, as I'm sure you do too.

In alphabetical order, here are a few recommendations:

- 99Bitcoins: Bitcoin in Plain English (www.99bitcoins.com)
- Bitcoin Magazine (www.bitcoinmagazine.com)
- Bitcoin News (www.news.bitcoin.com)
- Blockchain News (www.the-blockchain.com)
- BlockGeeks (www.blockgeeks.com)
- Brave New Coin (www.bravenewcoin.com)
- Coin Market Cap (www.coinmarketcap.com)
- CoinDesk (www.coindesk.com)
- Coinidol (www.coinidol.com)
- Coinjournal (www.coinjournal.net)
- Cointelegraph (www.cointelegraph.com)

- CryptoCoinsNews (www.ccn.com)
- Ethnews (www.ethnews.com)
- Let's Talk Bitcoin (www.letstalkbitcoin.com)
- NewsBTC (www.newsbtc.com)
- Reddit (www.reddit.com)
- Unitimes (www.unitimes.media)

GLOSSARY

This is a glossary of cryptocurrency terms that have come into use since the introduction of Bitcoin in 2009, as well as some financial trading and computing jargon you need to know to understand how it gets its value.

As with the rest of this book, by the time you read it this information may not include some of the latest developments. Nevertheless, it's a great base on which to build your understanding of crypto—and barring a similarly huge technological leap, the basic concepts are unlikely to change anytime soon.

And if that leap does happen, don't worry. We'll be on it (and ready to share it) faster than you can make your next trade.

Without further ado, here's the vocabulary you'll need to sound like a crypto pro, and know what you're talking about. Words in **bold** type are listed elsewhere in this Glossary.

Address (cryptocurrency)
An alphanumeric string of characters that makes up your unique **cryptocurrency** ID—the credential that allows you access to the cryptocurrency holdings in your name. **Blockchains** are the publicly accessible records of transactions from one address to another.

The same user can have multiple addresses, in the same way they can use different email addresses depending on the need.

Altcoin
Short for 'alternative coin', or any **crypto** other than **Bitcoin**. Examples include **Ether**, LiteCoin, Ripple, Dash and (at this writing) thousands more.

ASIC
Application-Specific Integrated Circuit, a device similar to CPUs and graphics cards. These use their processing power solely for mining and decrypting crypto in a **mining rig**.

Beauty/Beautiful
Miner slang for a released **Bitcoin block** that they have decrypted and is suitable for adding to Bitcoin's **blockchain**, granting them a share of its value.

Bitcoin (BTC)
The first **cryptocurrency**, introduced in 2009 by Satoshi Nakamoto and a small community of pioneers. It is the standard against which all others are measured; you'll generally see a list of attributes such as value, transaction speed, privacy and others that say how the **crypto** differs from Bitcoin itself.

Capitalised, 'Bitcoin' refers to the currency proper, while lowercase 'bitcoin(s)' refers to specific amounts of it. Today a single bitcoin is worth thousands of dollars, and trading of smaller amounts such as milli-bitcoins, micro-bitcoins or **satoshis** is more commonplace.

To resolve the limitations of Bitcoin as designed, hard **forks** in mid-2016 and late 2017 produced branching cryptocurrencies Bitcoin Cash (BCH) and Bitcoin Gold (BCG).

Block

A new entry to a **blockchain** ledger, consisting of the sending and receiving IDs, and the amount involved. New blocks are **mined** into circulation, with their payout (in the case of **Bitcoin**) halving every four years.

Blockchain

An encrypted, almost incorruptible ledger of transactions from one address to another that is attached to your user account, updated several times hourly—six times, in the case of **Bitcoin**.

This is the official record of what and how much (of potentially anything, not just **crypto**) you own, receive, sell or give away.

Caesar

Title of the Roman emperor in ancient times, used in this book as a personification of government authority.

Coin

See 'cryptocurrency'.

Crypto

Short for 'cryptocurrency'. It refers to the fact that cryptocurrencies begin as encrypted 'blocks' of data that must be decoded through **mining**—usually through application of vast amounts of computing power.

Cryptocurrency

A financial product (with a stock-like variable monetary value) consisting of recorded, permanent agreements between computers and user identities, with new units made available by **cryptography-breaking mining**. These are decentralised with records updated by everyone in the product's network, rather than controlled by a central bank. Attractive due to its pseudonymity and theoretical immunity to interference from governments.

Specific cryptocurrencies have come to be known as simply '**coins**' or '**tokens**'.

Cryptography
The science of secure, tamper-proof communication through encoding information in an unintelligible form, using a mathematical operation; to be decoded by the recipient's computer using a key sent to it, or else by brute-force guessing billions of solutions a second. The latter is the approach behind **crypto mining**.

DAO
A Decentralised Autonomous Organisation—that is, a group of Ethereum smart contracts written to serve a specific purpose.

Dark Web
The part of the Internet where hidden message boards, drug sales and other illegal activity flourish, accessible only through specially-built Web browsers designed not to leave an electronic 'trail' of their user history. Needless to say, it's popular with criminals and law enforcement agents.

Crypto is popular there due to its pseudonymous nature, but remember it's simply a tool—it's only as good or evil as the person using it. Not to be confused with the '**Deep Web**'.

Decentralisation
The distribution of authority and decision-making power throughout an entire organisation, creating autonomous units that work independently towards a common goal.

In the context of cryptocurrencies, this means users form a **P2P** network with no single point where it can be shut down.

Deep Web
The parts of the Internet that are accessible only to users with valid credentials, such as a user ID and password. Most Internet utilities such as online shopping accounts, email and many more are technically part of the Deep Web. Not to be confused with the 'Dark Web'.

Double-spending
The error of digital money being 'paid' to a recipient, while the sender can simply copy it and keep the money they supposedly 'sent'. The result is that the same sum of money can be spent over and over again.

ETF
Short for Exchange-Traded Fund, a fund that is traded like an ordinary stock but actually combines various shares chosen by its managers. It is widely believed that cryptocurrencies may eventually be traded this way.

Ether (ETH)
The traded cryptocurrency used to raise funds for, and run, new projects on **Ethereum**.

Ethereum
A blockchain environment envisioned as a 'world computer', where blockchain-based applications can be created and run, and money raised through pre-programmed **smart contracts**. Projects are funded using **cryptocurrency** known as **ether**, and allocate using a resource known as **gas**.

Exchange (cryptocurrency)
Similar to a stock exchange; a central online hub where **crypto** prices are tracked and you can order or sell specific quantities with **fiat**. Like in the stock market, some exchanges are more reliable than others.

Fiat
Actual money, such as US dollars, euros and other currencies. The term is used in the context of payment for amounts of **cryptocurrency**, and it is so-called because it is approved by government authority.

Fork
An operation that splits a **blockchain** into two separate ones, usually for technical reasons, such as the block size limit in **Bitcoin**. Forks can be 'soft' or 'hard'. In **crypto**, a soft fork retains compatibility with the existing **blockchain**, while a hard fork creates an entirely new **cryptocurrency** with no link to the old one.

FOMO
Fear Of Missing Out.

FUD
Fear, Uncertainty and Doubt.

Gas
A special unit used by **Ethereum** to measure the 'work' needed to perform a particular action, to ensure that the right amount of **ether** is paid to perform it.

Hash
A mathematics-based cypher used to encrypt data and ensure it is securely transmitted. New **crypto** units are released in a hashed form, and the act of providing computing power to break the hashes is known as **mining**.

Hash rate
A measure of a **mining rig**'s computing power, based on how many guesses at solving the **hash** it can make per second. A higher hash rate means faster guessing, and a higher chance of winning the race for the right to add to the **blockchain**.

Initial Coin Offering (ICO)
The initial sale of a percentage of custom-made **crypto** by a startup to investors, usually for public fundraising; the investors stand to gain if the new crypto is successful and rises in value. This is similar to a new company's first sale of its stocks, or an initial public offering (IPO).

Due to the fact that ICOs are open to the entire community, many startups opt for them rather than the more traditional model of venture capital.

Internet of Things (IoT)

An expression for the concept of linked items sharing information to make life more streamlined. For example, your driveway could have an IoT sensor to detect the arrival of your car, which then automatically turns on the connected air-conditioner and lights to welcome you home.

Lightning Network

A **cryptocurrency** transfer protocol that aims to make transactions instant, solving the delay in verifying them through miners.

Mining

The act of transacting by adding your computing power to efforts to decrypt 'blocks' of **crypto** as they are released. The computers that decrypt each **hash** are called **mining rigs**, and their owners ('miners') are rewarded if they are the first to complete the decryption.

Mining farm

A purpose-built facility where hundreds or thousands of linked computers are set up for mining **crypto** as quickly as possible, through combining their calculating power into a single, powerful **mining rig**.

More power means a higher chance of being the first to break the **hash** and earning the resulting payout. They profit by having their share of the mining proceeds exceed their prodigious operating costs, especially in the form of power bills, maintenance and cooling. Access to a farm's processing power is often sold on the Internet, with the promise of a share of the proceeds.

Mining rig
A computer running **cryptocurrency-mining** software.

Mint
Nakamoto's term for a bank or other financial authority that verifies transactions to be error-free. Not to be confused with the government mints that create physical notes and coins.

Nakamoto, Satoshi
Pseudonym used by the as yet unknown inventor (or inventors) of **Bitcoin, blockchain** and **cryptocurrency** as a concept. Several people and groups have been suspected of being Nakamoto, but no conclusive evidence has been found.

Open source
A license arrangement that makes software and the underlying source code freely available for anyone to use, modify and re-distribute as they see fit, without paying or needing permission from the original creators. This allows public users all over the world to study, adapt and collaborate on projects.

Several cryptos like **Bitcoin** and **Ethereum** are open-source, as are programmes like OpenOffice, a free alternative to Microsoft's Office suite of programmes.

Peer-to-peer (P2P)
A decentralised network of computers where every member can both request and carry out a service; the opposite of a client-provider model.

Pseudonymity
The property of online identities like **crypto addresses**, email or Facebook accounts; they do not have to be in your real name should you so choose. Some identifying information is still present, such as in **blockchain**—for example, the transaction history of your **Bitcoin address**.

Not to be confused with anonymity, which refers to a complete lack of identifying information.

Satoshi
Slang for the smallest tradeable unit of **Bitcoin**, named in honour of its creator. One satoshi is equivalent to one hundred millionth $(1/10^8)$ of a bitcoin.

Segregated Witness (SegWit)
A mid-2016 proposal to remove ('segregate') the identity (**SegWit**) check from each new **Bitcoin** transaction, to enable more transactions to be processed per minute.

Smart contract
An automated, pre-arranged series of transactions in **Ethereum** that is set to trigger when certain conditions are met. For example, a smart contract can be made to pay out amounts of **ether** to various parties when a purchase is confirmed.

Token
See **cryptocurrency**.

Wallet
Your secure user identity linked to your **address**, which determines your access to your own **bitcoins**. A hardware wallet might be used, in which a physical device connects to your computer via USB and authenticates your identity as well.

WannaCry
A viral attack on computers worldwide in early 2017, in which hackers seized victims' private documents, encrypted them and held them for ransom. Infamous in that the hackers only accepted ransom payments in **Bitcoin**, giving rise to concerns that **crypto**'s anonymity was giving criminals another useful tool.

Wiki
A shared article board that anyone in the community can edit. The word comes from Wikipedia, and is Hawaiian for 'quick'.

ACKNOWLEDGEMENTS

Thank you my dearest mom, FLY, for risking her whole life with one trade—me. That trade was funded with the help of my granny; the late Uncle Steve; the kindest Uncle Wai and the warmest Auntie Lai Yee.

I would like to specially thank my lovely wife, Hsin, for tirelessly guiding me in the right direction of life. You are the most selfless person in this world.

Xiao, Han and Jue, my three little ones, have been super supportive—yes, some of these wallets will go to you soon.

My previous bosses and mentors—I am nothing without you: Mark, Khoo, CK, David, Driss, David, Paul and more.

Stepping into the NUS Computer Science glass building in 2016 changed my life; I owe it to the profs and student friends I met there. Specially, Beng Chin and Gene Yan, thanks for the guidance.

For my book cover, I wanted to illustrate the initial stage of cryptocurrency and how Bitcoin will float out like a bubble and achieve clarity. Much thanks to my friend and artist, Aaron Gan for painting my vision.

Last but not least, my crypto comrades in Kyber Network and Digix Global. Thanks for allowing me to participate in these glorious projects.

ABOUT THE AUTHOR

Leng Hoe Lon, CFA serves as Executive Advisor of Kyber
Network (www.kyber.network), a decentralised cryptocurrency
exchange powered by Ethereum smart contracts and is also an
angel investor of Digix Global (https://digix.global), a company
that aims to tokenise physical assets and make them fungible on the
Ethereum blockchain in order to increase the pool of liquidity in
a decentralised marketplace. Before this, he was CEO of machine-
learning startup Shentilium Technologies, and co-founder of
trading and mentoring firm TrackRecord Asia.

Before his foray into entrepreneurship, his 19-year financial
trading career saw him holding the positions of Portfolio Manager
at Tudor Investment Corporation (2011-2016); CEO at Tudor
Capital Singapore (2013–2015); Managing Director at Goldman
Sachs (2007–2011); ABN AMRO (2004–2007); JP Morgan
(2003–2004); Deutsche Bank (1997–2003). He holds a Bachelor's
Degree in accounting and finance from the University of Warwick,
England.

ABOUT THE CO-AUTHOR

Pearlin Siow runs Boss Of Me, a boutique book-writing agency that specialises in helping people write as well as publish books. Together with her team of content specialists, she has written several bestselling biographies for top entrepreneurs and companies in Singapore. Her clients range from billionaires to stay-at-home mothers. Connect with her at www.bossofme.sg

ABOUT THE COVER ARTIST

Aaron Gan is the 2015 UOB Painting of the Year, Gold Award, Established Artist Category, Singapore winner. Born in Singapore in 1979, Gan graduated with a Bachelor of Commerce (Dean's List) from the University of Western Australia in 2003. In 2012, he gave up his corporate career to become a professional artist.

With his exuberant painting style, Gan has earned numerous sell-out shows under his belt. He showcases regularly in Singapore and internationally and his works have graced the collections of many corporations and institutions. He has also collaborated with many intenational brands. His website is https://aarongan.com

FUNDRAISING FOR SEEING IS BELIEVING

Leng Hoe Lon self-published a small print run of *Decrypted*. Through sales of the book to friends and family, he raised over $170,000 for Seeing is Believing (more info on SiB at the end of the article). Here is the back story behind the endeavour.

With nearly 20 years experience on the trading floor, Hoe Lon decided to explore how technology and data analytics could in the future take over trading jobs. Along the way he made new friends and learned more about blockchain and cryptocurrency. As a seasoned trader, he could see the endless possibilities but also realised that many people eager to make a quick buck but without sufficient knowledge could easily fall victim to scams and cheats.

This led him to write *Decrypted* which seeks to demystify this up-and-coming alternative investment class. He saw that the book could educate people and at the same time, he could use the book as a fund-raising opportunity for a charitable cause.

Why a charitable cause? Hoe Lon firmly believes that most people just need an opportunity or a leg-up to succeed in life. He considered various beneficiaries for his fund-raising efforts but in the end decided to support Seeing is Believing. He was already familiar with the work of SiB and he thought it was a good cause; to give someone another shot in life through the gift of sight. He was also inspired by his colleague Vishal Agrawal, a visually impaired trader in Mumbai; how Vishal managed to overcome blindness and be as efficient as his sighted colleagues. The icing on the cake was when Hoe Lon found out that Standard Chartered Bank would match any amounts raised for SiB, thus doubling the contribution to the charity.

Hoe Lon would like to thank his friends and family for their support and generous donations. A special shout out goes to his wife who has been his most dependable companion and cheerleader.

* * *

Seeing is Believing (SiB) is a long-standing collaboration between Standard Chartered and the International Agency for the Prevention of Blindness (IAPB). The IAPB is an alliance of civil society organisations, corporations and professional bodies promoting eye health through advocacy, knowledge and partnerships. The award-winning initiative, Seeing is Believing, is the result of two highly committed organisations combining relevant skills, resources and connections for the purpose of eliminating avoidable blindness. They partner with leading eye-care experts and non-governmental organisations (NGOs) to develop and deliver quality eye-care projects globally. Their partners understand the local healthcare issues impacting communities and how to respond to immediate and longer-term requirements. With an ambitious target to raise $100 million by 2020, Seeing is Believing is committed to help eliminate avoidable blindness and visual impairment.